LETTERS BEHIND BARS

A Mother-Son Memoir

CINNAMIN HERRING
BENJAMIN SIMMS HERRING, JR.

Contact www.cinnaminherring.com

ISBN 979-8-9851533-0-9 (paperback)

ISBN 979-8-9851533-1-6 (EPUB e-book)

ISBN 979-8-9851533-2-3 (hardcover)

Book design by Cinnamin Herring

Cover design by Cinnamin Herring

Cover painting by Cinnamin Herring

Letters Behind Bars

For Ben

AUTHOR'S NOTE

I wrote this memoir in collaboration with my oldest son, Benjamin Simms Herring, Jr. (Simms). All portions of this book were written by me, except letters addressed to "Mom" and other sections specifically attributed to Simms. Although this is a true story based on actual events and conversations, I used fictional names for some characters, including my younger son, whom I have called Rhett.

My younger son did not want to be included in this story, but his character demanded attention when his actions affected our family. I considered his request for privacy and did my best to tell only what was most relevant to the story. And although I cannot stop the truth from hurting, I want to love and forgive, as I have been loved and forgiven.

PREFACE

When this project first peeked its head into the world, I didn't recognize it as a book. In fact, the circumstances that led to writing this story started as a force that pulled me from the things I had planned. I realized I could argue to the end of the earth about my own rights. But without love in action, I believed everything in my life would be meaningless. And that truth put me back together when I fell apart. It brought me back when I ran. It compelled me to start and finish this project with my son, Simms. And it proved true when I argued against it.

I have never been inclined to surrender to dire circumstances, although they seem to have gotten the best of me a few times in the past. But those experiences taught me to hold joy close to my heart, like a precious jewel. It is a light I can shine through the darkness to find my way. It is a fire that warms me in the frozen tundra, or a tender caress that comforts a hurting heart. And, when necessary, it is a steel beam of sureness and direction. But this wasn't always so. It started, like anything, as a small flame that was easily put out by a gust of wild wind or a splash of wintry water—until one day, when I decided I would let nothing destroy my joy again. With immense gratitude for life and love, I vowed to steward with diligence the soul that abides within me.

For this reason, I was moved by the words of Ralph Waldo Emerson in his essay "Self Reliance." When unfortunate events threatened to steal my joy and my family, I determined I would not allow them to "be anything more than a cheerful apologue or parable of my being and becoming." Each morning, I would wake up and gather the remnants of my heart into a little bundle. I would caress it as I inhaled love and exhaled fear. With thanksgiving, I would accept my manna for the day and announce, "I have all I need." Then, I would write.

After several drafts of my first novel, I believed I had gained valuable knowledge about novel writing and improved my skills in that regard. However, my interest in someday publishing my novel waned in the light of changing circumstances. After my son's arrest, all I could think of was how to be a better mother for both my young adult sons. How could I express my love to them and be a positive influence in their lives?

I knew that my time of parenting them as children had passed. This season would look different. But how? I had been counting on Ben, my husband, to play a major role in their lives as young men, whereas I was the early childhood specialist. Before I became a mother, I had equipped myself to mother them as children, but I found that I was clueless about how to mother them as young men. It broke my heart into a million pieces every single day that I could not give them the thing I believed they needed most of all—their father.

Ultimately, I had to step up to the plate and figure things out, one moment at a time. This book results from my efforts to be a positive, loving influence on Simms—and indirectly on Rhett— who told me he did not want to be in this story or have a relationship with me. Subsequently, I tried to respect his wishes as much as possible. However, he was, and is, significant in my heart. Furthermore, I do not want to hurt him by what I have presented in this story. Instead, I tried to tell the story as accurately as I could while remaining mindful of his desire for privacy.

This is what I know. I have a positive and loving relationship with Simms. And throughout the various seasons of his addiction to opioids, he has never insulted or berated me, or slandered my name. He has not vandalized my home or property. Loving an addict does not coincide with allowing them to mistreat you. In my experiences, I have learned that a person can be an addict and still treat others with respect, love, and kindness. Sometimes, addiction causes good people to do questionable things, but addiction doesn't automatically make a kind person into a monster. Instead, some people allow negative aspects of their personality to dominate—either by feeding those propensities or dwelling on negative thoughts to justify their behavior. In those cases, I stand up for myself and make clear boundaries between me and that person while hoping for better times to come.

I love both my sons with a burning-hot, breathtaking, overwhelming, bring-me-to-my-knees kind of love. And they have both brought me to my knees, many times. Raising them has brought me pain—of course. But what outshines that by a million stars is the joy of knowing and loving them; the joy of living in a world where they exist; the joy of remembering their sweet baby faces, their tiny whimpers at my bosom, and their precious heartbeats against mine. Oh, the joy of their small footprints on the beach leading to grand castles of salty sand with little-boy voices tumbling in the wind. "Mom! Watch me!" And when their smallness was all worn out, I'd soak up the sweetness of bedtime stories and goodnight cuddles. All these memories sparkle like stars in the universe of my soul, warming my heart and reminding me that love is the one true thing.

In this book, Simms and I have shared our hearts and souls (minus much of Rhett's involvement) to present an authentic story that might encourage other families affected by addiction, incarceration, loss, or all of the above.

In early 2019, I was still trying to summon the attention and passion required to revise my novel, but concern for my sons pulled my heart and mind toward thoughts of how I might influence them in some positive way.

As I allowed love to wash over my heart, I saw a real story bubbling out from under my novel. It was a story about addiction and isolation, loss and heartache, love and dreams. And the story compelled me to search for whatever else might be there. What would I find about trust or tolerance? Was there any peace in recovery? Could joy even make an appearance in this story?

My heart pleaded over the apprehension that tried to paralyze me, "Please look and share what you find—for your family, and for the other people who want to look with you."

During one of our visits in late spring of 2019, I told Simms what was on my heart. He agreed that the story must be told. We had to make this all count. What mattered now was that Simms needed a purpose for life—and I did too, for that matter. My vision of the book I would publish had been clarified by traumatic, unforeseen events. With great relief, I submitted to fate, bundled up the mangled drafts of my fictional novel, and laid them to rest, knowing that all the writing and studying I had done served an important purpose in helping me find my voice and develop my writing style. I could let it go without feeling like I had failed.

With this realization, I decided that if Simms was not going to be able to earn a college degree in prison, we would do the next best thing. With a semester of basic courses under his belt from Cape Fear Community College, Simms agreed to embark on a comprehensive autodidactic education. I started sending books—some that he requested, and some that I thought were important. As the months crept by, our visits rolled over the hills of an eclectic educational landscape, and we both gleaned all we could from every moment of interaction.

When we could finally hug and talk in person without being

directly recorded, it was an important turning point for us—one that eventually created the fertile soil where our story would grow through a combination of letter correspondence, phone calls, and regular contact visits. First, the visits had been terrifying. Then, they had been challenging. But we kept coming to the table with honesty, love, and determination to make our conversations meaningful. And we kept writing.

This story is about hopes and dreams. It's about pushing through the hard stuff, loving and forgiving ourselves, being there for each other, and accepting differences. It's about moving past judgement to build trust. And it is about developing a vision, taking responsibility, expressing our ideas, cooperating, and accomplishing a dream. It is about two people proving to ourselves that we can set a goal and diligently work toward it one step at a time until we finally cross the finish line and accomplish what we set out to do.

Will it be the best thing I ever publish? Who knows? But I had to start somewhere. I will keep learning, working, and growing. I will keep creating, despite my insecurities; despite the voices in my head that say what I make is not good enough; despite the voices that say I should not even try. This book is about me loving someone and chasing the demon of fear down, facing her head-on, and setting her straight on who is in charge of my life.

In my determination to write and publish this book, I told fear a few things whenever she came to haunt me. "Fear, you are not in charge of my life, nor will you ever be. It is true that some people will not be interested in what I have written. Others may not like my style. But none of that matters. What matters is that I am compelled to write, and so it is part of my life's purpose. I know about all the talented writers, and I admire many of them. I recognize that I can never write like them. Instead, I will write like me. And I will not give up on my dreams!"

I want this book to show my sons that I did not let fear hold me back. People have asked, "Are you sure you should publish such a personal story?" and warned that others would judge me. These are reasonable concerns. Furthermore, I have considered them from every angle over the course of several years. What I know is that I was compelled to write this book. So, I wrote it honestly, with love and sincerity. Henceforth, I plan to keep creating as long as I have the ability to do so—as an offering of gratitude for life, joy, and love. Thank you for reading our story!

PROLOGUE

June 21, 2020

"Well, it's like this. If the truth was purty, they'da called it somethin' else," Wayne said as he contemplated the condition of my HVAC system.

When he first saw the damage to my thermostat, Wayne's brow furrowed as he shook his head. "I ain't ever seen nothin' like this. What the heck happened?"

"Apparently, a lacrosse ball hit it a while back, but the tenants didn't tell me about it."

Wayne laid the shattered thermostat aside and finished connecting a new one, tested the system a few times, and declared my air conditioner irreparable.

"If you woulda known about the thermostat when it happened, you mighta been able to get a few more years outta that unit." Wayne pursed his lips and shook his head as he tugged at worn blue jeans to cover the belly that had found its way out from under his sleeveless t-shirt. "It's a cryin' shame, but you're gonna need a whole new AC unit." Wayne plodded around the yard toward the main part of the system and showed me what was wrong. "Ya see here…" He pointed to some part like I would recognize it and explained how the neglected thermostat likely hastened the old unit to its grave by causing it to short-cycle until the compressor burned out.

I was too disappointed about the overall condition of my house to let emotions have a place. *Just take the blows and keep moving forward*, I told myself in a dazed state of disbelief.

Rhett, my younger son, was out of the nest—again. And this time, he would have to fly because the nest would not be open for returns anymore. Exhausted to the point of numbness, I had wished him well and said, "I hope you have a great life—somewhere else."

Later, I looked in my heart with curiosity, not wanting to find any bitterness there. And after steeping in despondency for a while, I sifted through the frustration and found pure love for my son. I picked up a dart of that love and sent it out into the universe to wherever he had gone. In my mind, I watched it nestle into his heart, and I was determined to believe and remember the beautiful things about him. But later, I learned I must remember the other things too. I could not deny the ugly truths or pretend they did not exist. Instead, I would stand over them with love for myself and for the man buried somewhere underneath all of Rhett's anger and judgment. I would believe in that man and imagine joy and peace for all of us.

As my eyes fell on those "other things," through wet lenses, I watched the salty drops of hope and love cover the ugliness that fear had brought there. A mound of unspeakable deeds was visible. But at that moment, I made the mound a grave.

Nothing can take my joy or my love, I thought, swallowing the burning ache that tried to overtake me. I pulled thick summer heat into my lungs and gathered whatever remnants of hope I could find scattered on the floor of my heart.

Wayne installed the new AC unit later that evening without complication, and I poured my heartache over the condition of my family into physical labor: scrubbing hardwood floors, washing cushion covers, and shampooing rugs. All the while, I warded off frustration about Rhett's resistance to my authority and instruction—which had contributed to the deterioration of the property.

I had to give him the chance to do it, I reminded myself. *I knew it might not work, but I had to let him try it on his own. This is all fixable.*

As all the episodes of the past few years rolled through my mind like a movie, I found comfort in knowing I had given him many opportunities to flourish. *I will not beat myself up over his choices. He has to find his way. I will not accept the blame for his problems. I have tried to do what Ben would want. Just because Rhett does not see any of it the way I do doesn't mean he is right.* I knew I had not been perfect, but I had been willing to keep trying, willing to love, willing to forgive and keep moving forward.

However, Rhett was not a child anymore. I could not just "ignore undesired behavior," as the books had suggested. I resolved that I would not tolerate abusive behavior from my adult son, no matter how much compassion I felt for him. He had lost his father and experienced significant trauma resulting from his brother's actions and consequences. And I mirrored all that pain as if it were my own. *But that doesn't justify hostility and destruction,* I concluded. *He can go his own way until he decides to be civil.*

The following morning, I awoke with a sense of satisfaction at having charge over my property again. My sons were heavy on my heart because it was Father's Day. In addition to my own grief for Ben, I felt deep sadness for my sons and their loss of a father. But when the pangs of sorrow pricked at my heart that day, I stifled my emotions by doing the next thing that needed to be done—over and over.

First, I collected furniture and other items that had been cluttering my home and mind. After placing them on the front porch, I sent a message to Rhett telling him to take what he wanted.

Then, I turned my attention to Ben's guns, which had been a continual source of contention between me and Rhett. He believed the guns were his, even though his father had left the decision to me. Considering Ben's intentions, I started out trying to take care of the guns until a time when I imagined Rhett would be ready for the responsibility of owning them. But Rhett's tantrums wore me down. He wanted the guns and resented my control over them. And since hunting with the guns had been a special father-son activity, I could not find peace in selling them because of the sentimental value they held. Ultimately, I did not want to keep the guns in my house day after day while Rhett boiled over it.

So, I disregarded my opinion that he should earn the guns— or at least show some respect to receive them. I relinquished Ben's guns to Rhett and let relief fill the space they had occupied in my mind. Two days later, the old floorboards of my house cried their sighs of relief too when Pete from the local pawn shop hoisted the massive gun safe onto his truck and drove away. I was finally free from the guns and the oppressive air that lingered around them—I hoped.

Minutes later, my phone rang. Caller ID showed Mountain View Correctional Institute, so I took a deep breath, answered with a swipe, and listened to an automated message that told me my conversation would be recorded.

Like a deer sensing the aim of a hunter's rifle, everything inside me said, "Run!" except my heart. Would I find the courage to stand over fear for the sake of my family—for love?

PART I

"Even
After
All this time
The Sun never says to the Earth,
'You owe me.'
Look
What happens
With a love like that,
It lights the whole sky."
—Hafiz

CHAPTER 1

March 2015

When the phone vibrated on my desk in the back room, I recognized the number and walked away into the kitchen to refill my water bottle, resisting the pull in my heart to answer. I closed my eyes and pushed the pain down into some deep crevice, hoping it would stiffen like mortar and hold my heart together. I stood at the counter, willing the emotions to seep out through my clammy skin.

Silence.

I thought the moment had passed until I heard the faint vibrations of my phone pulsing through the wall again. After two more tries, it was finally over—for the time being.

I went back to my desk and tried to finish one of many assignments that would be due over the next few days. I was numb as one side of my life butted firmly against the other, each determined to hold a place at the table of relevance. Half of me was a woman drumming at my dreams, and the other half was a mother foraging fragments of a crumbled heart. I felt the demon of fear laughing somewhere in the dark of that night, and my anger boiled. After my homework was done and the day's duties were complete, I double knotted my tennis shoes and bounded outside for my nightly run.

"I'll catch you, motherfucker!" I yelled down the street to the demon, not caring who heard my crazy rant. "And when I do, I'm going to beat the hell out of you!"

I ran until my legs gave out and sobbed into the grass of my front lawn until my emotions were exhausted. As I stared at the black pavement, I consoled myself by imagining that I had trampled the cruel demons on the street. All that remained was the rush of blood through my boiling veins and a salty crust of love and pain upon my cheeks.

January 2015

Simms was living with his girlfriend near the university while attending classes at Cape Fear Community College. They came by the house one evening, and Ben asked what they were up to later. When Simms told his father he was planning to meet up with someone from the past whom Ben knew, the conversation became heated.

"That girl is trouble, Simms," his dad said with stern urgency, hoping that Simms would heed his warning.

Later that evening, we got the call that Simms had been arrested on twenty-two drug-related charges. The girl he had met up with was part of a sting operation, and Simms got stung in a life-altering way.

Immediately after his arrest, Simms began experiencing withdrawal from his heroin addiction, but I did not know at that time he was addicted—or that he had ever used heroin. Consequently, our phone interactions were confusing and upsetting. During his incarceration, every visit and phone conversation was recorded. So, as bad as things were, we could not talk openly about anything that might jeopardize the pending case against him, including his struggles with addiction and withdrawal.

On top of that, I had no personal experience with heroin addiction—other than as a child with my father. And I never knew the details of his addictions. I only knew that his regular abuse of alcohol and various other mind-altering substances resulted in a slew of negative consequences for everyone in his orbit, including me. So, between my limited experience with addiction and our major communication barrier, I remained in the dark about the extent of Simms's personal struggle until he was released from the county jail in the fall of 2015.

However, I was aware that he had abused drugs. It had been a constant struggle within our family over the course of his teenage years. I had taken him to a number of doctors, various drug treatment organizations, and counselors—all to no avail. Eventually, I had encouraged him to attend a rehabilitation program at Port Human Services. Unfortunately, after only a few weeks at Port, he had been dismissed from the program for his unwillingness to participate in the required activities and his refusal to follow the rules of the facility.

That was when I finally realized he would have to be intrinsically motivated to work through a drug treatment program. I could do the work to get him in one and encourage him to say he would comply, but the only way he would ever benefit from a recovery program was if he believed it could help him and personally committed himself to it.

So, when he was arrested on an array of charges, some of which were felonies, I hoped that his incarceration would induce the intrinsic changes necessary for his successful recovery. For this reason, I did not plan to bail him out of jail. Later, when we found out that his bond was set at $125,000, it made the decision easier, from a logical perspective. I would not risk our livelihood to give him temporary relief from inevitable consequences.

Although all the details of our initial conversations are no longer clear in my memory, I recall the desperation, the denials, and the pleas for help because each cry triggered my mother bear instinct so acutely that I thought my heart might truly tear open and bleed out.

"Isn't there something you can do?" Simms's voice was strained with urgency, and my hands began to sweat as I felt the push of his words and the pleading spaces between them.

"I sent an email to your attorney." I reached up to press on a tight ball of muscles in my shoulder. "Looks like he has a pretty good reputation." I had been up late the night before working at my computer, and my body was screaming for relief.

"Well, I wish he would hurry up and come here," Simms snapped through the static in the phone lines. The phones at the county jail were known for extraneous crackling, and it was difficult to understand what he said.

"Your dad made some calls. The fees are pretty steep for a private attorney, and they don't want to make any guarantees. It's a tough case." I inhaled deeply, trying to settle my racing heart. *I have to be strong,* I thought, overwhelmed with responsibilities from all angles.

"The guys in here said it might take over a year to get the labs back. Please talk to him and tell him we need to get the labs back. That's gonna clear me."

"The what?" I strained to make out all the words between the crackling sounds.

"The labs!" Simms yelled, equally frustrated.

"Oh, yeah. I hope the results come back soon." I didn't know what to believe. Even though Simms was hoping the lab results would save him, my gut told me that would not be enough.

"Can you and Dad come see me?" Simms's voice shook, and I could hear that he was holding back tears as his voice faded to a whimper. "Please help me, Mom. There has to be something you can do. I was wrongly arrested. We need the labs back.

Please talk to the attorney. Please get me out of here! I have to get out of here!"

The desperation in Simms's voice pounded at me, merging itself with the beating of my heart until they were one thing—a burning, stinging, hurting, helpless pounding—pushing blood and an overdose of cortisol through my traumatized veins.

We listened to the static announcement that we would be disconnected in thirty seconds. My lips pursed, determined to suffocate the coals that seared on my tongue.

"Oh, yeah, and please send me books to read," Simms said. "All they have in here is a Bible and a few tattered books that everyone fights over. I'm going crazy in here! Mom, you have to believe me! I should not be here. This is all wrong."

"Then why did you break the smoke detector in the cell?" I asked.

"It was an accident! It was because…" His voice trailed off desperately, as if his words were chisels, chipping away at the injustice of his incarceration.

Scalding blood throbbed in my veins. Like lava, it oozed through me with suffocating finality. My lungs pulled at the surrounding air. But their efforts were no match for the force that squeezed my chest closed. I held the reins of my angry words and turned them on myself in silence. How could I have failed this miserably? My heart tumbled to the floor and shattered into a thousand shards of devastation.

"I'm sorry that you…" I started, but the call disconnected.

Musty air that had thickened in my lungs broke free, giving way to the heaviness of my son's circumstances, which engulfed me like a tidal wave. Our conversation was a tumultuous storm tearing through my mind as I wondered what to do—and what not to do.

"God, please help me," I cried out as I imagined being nineteen years old, seeing the doors of my future slammed and bolted.

Anger and frustration smoldered in my gut and tried to catch fire as watercolors of love simultaneously washed over me, blurring everything into a muddled mess of inadequacy. Hadn't I blamed myself enough over the years?

That doesn't work, I reminded myself. *It is not my fault. It cannot be my fault. I can't fix this. Simms has to fix it,* I demanded, trying to convince myself that I was in control of my own life.

My insides were shredded as I looked down at the picture in my anatomy book, trying to activate something in my brain, hoping I could pass the test I was scheduled to take in an hour. I felt like I couldn't remember anything. My brain had short-circuited.

Somebody has to hold it together, I thought, closing my throat on the emotions trying to climb out. I stared at the illustration on the page in front of me and focused all my attention on the intricate anatomy of the larynx and pharynx.

"Trachea, thyroid cartilage, cricoid cartilage, vocalis muscle, ventricle, epiglottis, hyoid bone..." I spoke the words aloud with insistence, as if they were a chant to ward off demons.

When my vision was sufficiently blurred, I gave up on studying and slid to the floor, where I wrapped myself into a ball and submitted to emotion as it engulfed me like a rip current and pulled me out to sea.

But responsibility was waiting on the shore, so I found my way back and went to take my anatomy exam. With two years of a three-year graduate program in communication sciences and disorders completed, I was well on my way to finishing an academic program that would qualify me to practice speech-language pathology.

My goal of earning a master's degree had developed after I took a children's literature class during my undergraduate studies at the University of Houston. I decided I wanted to be a writer and subsequently realized that I might need a graduate degree in order to be taken seriously within that domain. At the time, I was newly married to my late husband, Ben, who was fifteen years my senior. In light of his age, we decided to have our children a few years after I finished my bachelor's degree—when he was forty and I was only twenty-five.

More than a decade later, when both our sons were in high school, I sat down with Ben and discussed my vision for the next phase of our life. Our nest would be empty in a few years, and I wanted Ben to be able to retire early because he had worked long and hard for many years.

"If I go to graduate school and become a speech-language pathologist, I could practice travel therapy. You could retire and I could take jobs in whatever places we want to visit. Then, I can continue working without being stuck in one place in a classroom," I suggested. "And you can play a little more."

Ben agreed that it was a good plan and decided he would take a step toward retirement at the end of 2015. By that time, I would have earned the necessary credentials for my career change from teaching to language therapy, and we would be on our way to making the best of our "golden years."

CHAPTER 2

Even though I had the dream of being a writer, I was the practical sort when it came to home and family. I believed it was important, for the sake of my family, to have a predictable and relatively certain income. This meant I would need to allow my dreams room to grow in the spaces between what was best for my family. For this reason, I chose a field of study that could take me toward both my goals. Earning a master's degree in communication sciences and disorders could qualify me for a profession that was in high demand, while adding to my qualifications as a writer.

February 2015

"I'm going to see Simms tomorrow," I announced one evening as Ben poured a generous glass of merlot and plodded to his chair.

"Well, I can't see my namesake in jail. I just can't do it," Ben mumbled, shaking his head and staring at the floor with weary eyes. He leaned forward and put his head in his hands, let out a long sigh and said with a trembling voice, "Tell him I love him."

I stood by his chair and ran my fingers through his soft gray curls, wishing that I could soothe his sadness.

"I will."

The next day, I navigated the long hallways of New Hanover County Jail to see Simms.

"Your dad is taking things pretty hard, as you might imagine. He couldn't come this time, but you know he loves you," I told Simms through the crackling jail phone we had to talk on during our visit. The glass partition between us had wires running through it that made Simms look like an animated puzzle. My heart begged me to tell him his father would visit soon, but I could not. "It's just hard for him to see you like this," I held the phone receiver with my shoulder and pulled at a frayed cuticle, willing away the wetness that blurred my vision.

Simms pleaded for me to do something and offered several suggestions about how I might help with his case, but I was drained from years of trying to get through to him. News of his arrest and related serious charges had plunged into my heart and syphoned off the faith I needed to fight for him. *I have to leave him in jail and let the chips fall because nothing else has worked.* I thought. *Maybe this will save him.* All I could do was hope something could save him because I had already tried everything I knew.

A letter from Simms to his father arrived before Ben's sixty-first birthday in 2015. He left it lying on the table beside his chair, but we did not talk about it. I could feel his sadness through the bottles of red wine in the trash and the silence that shrouded our home. How I wished I could take the pain away from him—and from Simms. I longed to understand what was happening and how to make things better.

March 2015

Dear Dad,

Where do I even begin? I really am quite ashamed to be stuck in here on your birthday. I am ashamed to be here, period, but being kept from you on your birthday feels especially shameful. I'm sure you don't feel respected or appreciated by me, and I regret the picture I have painted. This may be hard to believe. Certainly, current circumstances do not make it any easier, but I really do, with all my heart and soul, respect you more than anyone else in this world. Throughout my entire life, you have served as no less than the perfect role model for me. Sometimes, through deliberate instruction, other times by simply engaging in casual conversation with me.

Intentional or not, over time, the morals and virtues I have learned from you have built the foundation of who I am, and even more so, who I will become. I am sure I feel the same way about you as you do about your father. Therefore, I hope I can make you feel that I respect you as much as I really do. I can't wait to spend time with you when I get out there, doing anything, really. Through all the disrespect and injustices I have ever served you, you have still stood by my side and proven, beyond a shadow of a doubt, that you are my strongest advocate and the best friend I have ever had—or will have. My gratitude to you is boundless. I am eager to make you proud and prove that I won't let your name go to waste. I am exceedingly proud to bear the name that I do. I couldn't have asked for more from a father. You always go above and beyond. And I hope that, one day, I can be half the father you have been to me.

Send my love to Mom and Rhett—and to the rest of the family. And, of course, it goes out to you. Happy birthday, Dad! Have a good one for me.

With love and respect,

Your sometimes inconsiderate but genuinely regretful son,

Benjamin Simms Herring, Jr.

XOXOXOXO

P.S. I really do recognize how much you know what you're talking about, and I have seen firsthand how you are dead correct about the things you talk about—a fact I expect will become more apparent as I continue to mature. I love you, Dad.

~

Late March 2015

"We can't get him out," I said, with hot throbs of blood pounding into my ears.

"It's too much," Ben said. "He can't stay there." He stood motionless, staring into the backyard. A shiny film covered his eyes, threatening to erupt. I could not look, could not let myself think about the visions there, the memories of innocent years gone by. "I need to fix this," he muttered. "It's my fault. I should have told him."

"Told him what?" I asked, closing the dishwasher and walking around the bar to face him. He looked over at me, fixing his eyes on the railing of the back porch where two squirrels were squabbling over the peanuts he had put there the night before.

"How not to get caught," he said to the empty railing. "I knew he was being stupid. But how could it be right to teach him that?"

"We did our best. That has to be enough," I said, trying to convince myself, knowing I had to believe it to survive.

But it was not enough.

The regrets I had promised myself never to have ensnared me, sinking their bitter thorns deep into my skin. An orange glow faded in the sky, giving way to the cool darkness of a March evening. Ben carried a mug of beer to his recliner. I wiped countertops and straightened pictures on the walls, looking for some secret door of escape from the unresolved silence stretching its thin skin over the evening, swelling with wordless emotion over the black night. I wanted to tell him he was the best father in the world and assure him that it wasn't his fault, but I knew whatever I said would roll off his ears like water off a waxed boot. I could see the words already—dead on the floor.

I sat down on the couch and stared at the ball game on the screen while the words on the floor grabbed at me like ghost hands rising from some hell below. I lifted my feet and tucked them under my legs, watching from the corner of my eyes for any sign that Ben was still there in the room. He jumped and yelled something at the television as he tried to get the game to go his way.

A silent prayer ached in my heart for him. *Please let something—anything—go his way.* Meanwhile, my best friend had retreated completely into his stone cave, where I was a shadow on the wall.

I knew he was pretending to ignore me, hoping I would go away so that he could keep his emotions in check. And I did not want to provoke anything, but I knew he was at the edge of what he could take. I could feel the sinking of his heart from across the room. The anger inside me grew hotter, expanding like the trapped fire of a waking volcano. Ben deserved to enjoy life. He had worked long hours for as many years as I had known him. After years of frugality, it was supposed to be time for him to relax and play more. I could see the numbers lining themselves up in his head, and I knew he was seriously considering bailing Simms out of jail. With my limited understanding of how bail and bonds worked, I thought that would mean a second mortgage on the house, or some other drastic measure, considering Simms's extravagant bond of $125,000.

My skin grew hot and sticky, and the rock in my stomach turned at the thought of him not being able to retire at the end of the year as he had planned. This is officially catastrophic, I thought as my head spun for a solution. Before I knew what was coming out of my mouth, I heard the words as if someone else were saying them.

"If you get him out, I'm leaving," I said in desperation, having no intention of doing so.

My motive was only to say something with enough power to let Ben know this was not up for negotiation. We all experience the consequences of our own actions, no matter what anyone else pays. My gut told me that all the money in the world would not get Simms out of this predicament. If anything, paying money to get him out on bond would perpetuate the cycle of deviance and subsequent consequences.

I understand that my refusal to rescue my son might seem like a cold approach, but I knew with all my heart that getting him out at that time was not the answer. Nevertheless, immediately after those horrible words fell from my lips, the air in the room froze solid. I knew he understood. I needed him to trust me, and my stance gave him permission to blame me. We had put so much love and effort into equipping our sons.

Was it all in vain? I wondered as the only prayer I knew anymore played on repeat in my heart. *God, please help us.*

The phone rang, and I saw that it was Simms calling from the county jail. I silenced it and put my phone down on the kitchen counter, shielding myself from the sharp rings I could still feel pulsating through the quiet room. I gulped thick air, trying to swallow my anger. But it was slipping, giving way to sprouting cotyledons of love that wanted to hope and believe.

CHAPTER 3

March 2015

The tension in our home mounted as I tried to keep up with my graduate courses, Ben tried to pay attention to his work, and Rhett ran wide open with friends and sports. All the while, a sadness clawed incessantly on the walls of our home, digging its talons into all we had built, threatening to destroy our family.

"How can you just go about your day like nothing's wrong? It's like you don't even care," Ben accused.

As I tried to stay afloat in graduate school, the elephant in our house stood like a cold statue, ignored and unattended, for a time.

March Madness was getting underway, and I was glad for the distraction it offered. Ben would be immersed in the tournament all month, waiting for the relief of spring. Winter had been torturous, as the bitter cold of our son's incarceration threatened to remain indefinitely.

I turned toward him and stared, my mind spinning in an effort to process what his words meant. *After more than a quarter of a century together, how can he think I don't care?* I thought, flabbergasted.

I stood between him and the television, hoping he would

engage in a conversation. "I refuse to give someone else the power to ruin my life," I said.

With brows furrowed, he snapped back, "You don't act like it's affecting you at all!"

There was so much I wanted to say, but none of it would be enough. If all the years of living as truly as I could with him had not shown him the depths of me, what could? I thought he knew me. I had to get past this blow, past his belief that I was not affected by our son's plight.

While the reality of his incarceration and possible imprisonment marinated, Simms became progressively more desperate and erratic in his communications with us as he experienced post-acute withdrawal syndrome (PAWS). At that time, I did not know Simms was addicted to heroin. Nor did I know he was affected by PAWS, a condition with psychological and emotional symptoms that come and go for several months or more after withdrawal from an addictive substance. Following a heated phone conversation with Simms, bewilderment overwhelmed me and found its way onto the pages of a letter. I showed it to Ben before I mailed it, hoping that it would reveal something to him about how the ordeal was affecting me.

"Should I mail it?" I asked him, trying to initiate a discussion.

"Whatever you think, Champ," he said, laying the letter down and turning up the volume on whatever ball game was on.

I experienced his emotional pain like a constant strike to my own heart. I knelt in front of him and slipped my arms around his warm body. With my head against his heart, I felt the ache of our burden swell inside me and erupt as hot tears from tired eyes. I could not comfort him, so I went to the back room and sobbed into my pillow.

March 30, 2015

Dear Simms,

First of all, you must be recalling a conversation with someone else about God helping those who help themselves. Perhaps it was a conversation you had with yourself. I'm quite sure you haven't listened to a word I've ever said, so it cannot be my words you remember. Anyway, I never said that because I am well aware that the Bible doesn't say it like that.

Secondly, you have plenty of books you can re-read, and I'm quite sure you haven't memorized the books you have there. Nor have you memorized the Bible. Therefore, you have plenty to keep you occupied. Also, I don't plan on making sure you are entertained the whole time you are in jail. You have a mind, and you are capable of figuring out how to occupy it without someone else providing you with infinite entertainment. Maybe you should contemplate some of what you have already read.

As for your calls, I am not answering the phone because I don't have anything to talk about with you. I put all of my abilities and effort into raising you, loving you, and trying to be a good mother. Now, it is up to you to be who you decide to be. You are no longer my responsibility. I continue to have goals for myself. And right now, I need to stay focused on my goals. I love you and hope you get your life figured out, but I am not going to figure it out for you.

It is my opinion that I provided you with a good deal of quality experiences and education in order to equip you for a prosperous life. How you use these tools is up to you. I do not plan to let you suck the life out of me. I know you are not trying to do this, but I need you to recognize that you are not a child anymore. You have the power to be a blessing and encourage others, make an honest living, and much more. It's time to realize that the world isn't here to serve you (and that includes me). You are here to do something amazing, but it will never happen as long as I come along picking up all the pieces of your life and putting them neatly back in your toy box.

Right now, your body, soul, and mind are your home. You need to spend time in YOUR HOME contemplating, tidying, planning, memorizing, creating, and organizing. Then, you will be ready to accomplish your purpose and reach out to others—to OFFER something to the world. You will never be happy taking, and it will push others away. I could send you an endless supply of books, but this would only entertain you momentarily. Ultimately, you would not spend time tidying your own soul. This is why I am not sending you any more books. Furthermore, it's disgraceful to think you would ask for and accept a book from your friend who is on a very tight budget. Stop using people! Start spending time trying to learn something from them. You can learn from every person you encounter. It is not dependent on how smart they are. It is dependent on your perception.

It is one thing to be confident but quite another to think you know more than anyone you encounter. You are not the only intelligent person on the planet. And IQ certainly doesn't correlate to success or happiness. When you take more than you give, it wears people out. Eventually, some people realize that if they want to keep moving forward, they must leave some things behind. You are welcome to move forward with me, but I do not plan on staying behind with you. When you were a child, it was my duty to be your guide. But now, you are grown. I hope and pray you will discover abundant life. I also hope to be a part of your life. But this will depend on whether you decide to move forward, because that is where I am going.

Clearly, being your biggest fan wasn't a successful tactic. So, since I do not make a habit of doing the same thing over again and expecting different results, I'm trying something different— straight up honesty. You need to get it together. Start acting like there is someone else in the world besides yourself and take responsibility for your own life. We owe you nothing. And I don't plan on giving you anything else until you stop asking and start using all that you have already been given. I gave all I knew how to give for your entire childhood. I wasn't perfect, but I sure gave it a good try. So, use what I gave you. And if you don't remember what it was, maybe you were not paying attention. Maybe you ignored or discounted what I gave, thinking it was irrelevant. Now, you need to search your memories for what your family gave you. You need to find it and use it.

May your life get better. I want the best for you, as I always have. But I'm just feeling quite done with expending valuable effort on someone who, quite honestly, appears to be throwing out the most important things I'm giving and only keeping what seems useful, easy, and entertaining. I'm at my wit's end with you. I don't plan to make any space for your childish antics. Either grow up or find a life without me in it.

I said goodbye to my father because he was a user and never stopped sucking whatever he could get out of people. I didn't want him to hurt you, Rhett, or your dad. So, we parted ways. I always loved him because he was my father, but I could not help him.

Now, you and I are at the same crossroad. I will not live my days out having a son who comes around when he needs something and sucks the life out of his family and friends. I will not! You will not use us; take from us; expect our help, support, love, money, etc.; insinuate that it is your proper inheritance; or play on our emotions. When you are free again, you will either behave like the gentleman I know you are capable of being or find an option that doesn't involve me or Rhett. I cannot speak for your father to every extent, but he also deserves some peace. I will protect those I love at all costs, even if it means protecting them from others I love.

Sincerely,

Your mother

P.S. You probably better start getting up for breakfast again.

∽

Although winter began to loosen its grip and give way to spring, Ben's spirit continued to descend, and my mind rattled desperately for a way to help him.

"You need another hunting dog," I said. "Somebody that'll listen to you and mind you. It could be just what you need right now."

Ben took a deep breath and sighed despondently, "Maybe you're right."

CHAPTER 4

April 4, 2015

A couple of weeks later, Ben called me up to his office and showed me pictures of some Labrador pups he had found online.

"Let's go look at them!" I yelped, joyful at the thought of his emergence from the darkness.

"Tomorrow is Easter," he said. "But maybe we can go next week."

"Why can't we go today?" I asked as a sense of urgency fluttered in my gut.

Ben rubbed his beard with one hand and clicked through the pictures on his computer again. "Well, I guess I could give the guy a call."

"Yay!" I cheered, smiling and jumping with my hands up.

Less than an hour later, we were dressed and ready for our day trip to Pollocksville, North Carolina. Ben bustled around excitedly, preparing the motorcycle and packing his daily essentials. When he pulled the motorcycle out of the garage, I grabbed my helmet and stuffed a snack into my purse, ready for whatever adventure the trip would offer. We both felt good about the decision to adopt a hunting dog. It would give Ben a much-needed distraction, a new purpose, and a buddy; it would be something he could count on through the volatile season of parenting teenage boys.

The air was misty on that warm Saturday morning as the engine purred under me. BMWs are known for their quiet sophistication on the road, and the sound was comfortable to my ears. A few years back, Ben had traded his Suzuki for something that gave me more support in the back. He was always thinking of me, even when he wished he wasn't, I guess.

We had decided to take the motorcycle to Pollocksville on faith. Ben said the skies would clear up, and I couldn't resist saying yes to the adventure, longing for the joy he exuded when we rode together. It was our way of dancing since Ben did not care for dancing the conventional way.

Remembering back to our wedding day, a month shy of twenty-four years earlier, I had asked Ben for a second dance after the proverbial wedding dance, but he refused. I cried in the bathroom, afraid I had made a mistake by marrying him. But whether we were married or not, I knew I didn't want to live without him. Early in our relationship, I struggled with our age difference, wondering how I ended up in love with someone fifteen years my senior. But I was lovestruck, and there was no help for it. His gaze pierced my heart with unbreakable tethers. Who could say that he would die first just because he was older? Nobody, of course. Anything could happen. I loved him regardless of age. If I chose to walk away at any point, I would feel the loss. On the other hand, if I chose to make a lifetime plan with him, at least we could experience whatever fate had to offer. I decided that would have to be enough because my love for him did not want to let go—ever.

On the back of the BMW, I scooted closer to Ben and wrapped my arms around his waist. We pulled away from the drive with a feeling of hopeful anticipation for the sunshine we imagined—and for the joy of young innocence in a Labrador pup.

Ben's iPod streamed proudly through the speakers with the playlist from his sixtieth birthday party. "Swingtown" boomed in my ears, creating a moment of nostalgia. The bump at the edge of the driveway adjusted me in my seat, and the Steve Miller Band reminded me to breathe deeply and appreciate the adventure, despite the dull pain in my neck that had tempted me to ask about taking the truck instead.

Ten short minutes later, the sun was bright above us, and there was nothing in the world but that wonderful moment. The mist of threatening rain sparkled as the sun broke through, fighting for its right to rule over the day while the motorcycle purred beneath me. Fresh coastal air poured into my lungs as we gained speed on the open road. And I saw the fragility of life, floating around us like an angel. Sitting on the back of the bike, I was lured closer by Ben's tenderness until my inner thighs met his backside and my arms rested on his hips. Emotion swelled in my lungs and escaped from my eyes into the warm, hopeful wind of spring. Colorful blossoms of the season waved their greetings as we passed them. And the joy that radiated from Ben as we shared the simple pleasure of riding in the open wind eased my pain, both physically and mentally. That day, we were not just existing; we were living.

When we arrived in Pollocksville, the sun was high in the Carolina blue sky. It had burned away the clouds, and the air vibrated with sounds of spring along the country road that led us to the pups. A man came out of a house to greet us as we dismounted the motorcycle. Minutes later, five-week-old puppies were bounding around us curiously. I inhaled the summer air, savoring the sweetness of yelping pups and freshly cut grass. One of the smaller female pups came up to me, sniffing and whimpering. I was impressed with her graceful manners and decided she would be our new baby girl. Since the breeder would only guarantee the health of the pups after they were six weeks old, we arranged to return the following week.

Ben and the breeder were about the same age and found a lot in common right away. They talked about hunting, boating, and motorcycle riding. They shot the bull for a while, laughing and sharing stories. By the time we climbed on the bike to head back home, westerly trees had started to cast long shadows across the road. Hopeful with the idea of soon having a pup to lighten the weight of our current reality, we rode back toward Wilmington, enthusiastic about college basketball. The 2015 championships were wrapping up, and the final four teams would face off that night.

A few minutes after we left Pollocksville, Ben stopped at an intersection and got off the bike. I got off too, wondering what was going on, as this was not something I had ever seen Ben do before. It was not a busy intersection, but there were other cars around. I scanned the area to determine if it was safe to stay there, not sure what I would do if it wasn't. When I saw that cars were going around slowly, I turned my attention to Ben. He was walking around, shaking his leg.

"What's wrong?" I asked.

"Got a cramp," he said with a grimace and more leg shaking.

I handed him my water bottle, and he drank a little. After a couple more minutes, we got back on the bike and started toward home again. He assured me he was okay and stopped at the next gas station. We stayed there a few minutes while he hydrated and walked around some more without saying a word. I watched, evaluating. When he got back on the bike, I climbed on behind him with complete trust in his decision to continue.

Forty-five minutes later, we were home. Ben was silent, so I figured he didn't want to talk about what happened. I went inside to study for final exams and finish an assignment. The demands of graduate school consumed me most of the time, but the end was in sight, with only two semesters between me and the master's degree I had put off to raise the boys.

Ben changed into his bicycling garb (black spandex biking

shorts and a neon-yellow shirt). He said a quick goodbye down the hallway, telling me he was headed around the loop. About an hour later, he came in through the garage into the kitchen for some water. I pushed back from my computer and walked down the hallway from the bedroom to greet him.

As I turned the corner to the kitchen, I asked, "How was the wind?"

This was my standard question because it was an important element of the ride for him. He kept an ugly orange flag in the front yard to monitor the direction of the wind and based his riding plans on its forecast.

Ben looked up from his position in front of the refrigerator as if he was prepared to give me a rundown, but the words never came as he stepped toward me, fell to one knee, and crashed with blunt force onto the wooden floor, facedown.

I had never before seen Ben fall. My pulse raced to high alert. I called to him and watched him gasp for air. I was confused; my mind went everywhere at once, trying to come to a logical conclusion. He was unresponsive. I ran to the back room to get my phone and dialed 911. My heart pounded fast and loud, exploding an alarm through my veins.

I fell to my knees beside Ben and watched him gasp for air, trying to be patient with the 911 process. His 220-pound body was sprawled through the doorway from the kitchen to the hallway. The woman on the other end of the 911 call helped me determine that I needed to administer CPR. It was confusing because, since he was breathing at times, I thought he might have only fainted—and that he might recover without intervention.

Questions tumbled in my mind like numbers in a bingo cage. *Heat stroke? Allergic reaction?* When I determined he was not responding or regaining any regular breathing pattern, I started to turn him over, but saw there was not enough space in the threshold where he had fallen.

I dropped the phone on the floor to free my hands for the emergency and ignored the woman's voice as it shouted, "Ma'am, I can't hear you."

I had already told her what she needed to know—the address and the urgency of the situation. So, I ignored her demands to pick up the phone and focused on how to save Ben. Once she agreed with me that I needed to administer CPR, I knew I had to turn him over. Floating above the problem in some other dimension, I grabbed Ben's feet and pulled with all my might to get him to the open area of the kitchen floor. The urgency pushed me through the thick weight of time as I kneeled and pulled Ben's shoulder and side toward me with all my might. His body had gained all the weight of someone in deep slumber, and I knew I had to get him on his back to start CPR.

My blood was a clock, striking my temples at record speed, demanding that I accomplish what I knew I must. I grabbed the neon shirt he was wearing and wrapped it around my hands for a better grip, pulled all the air from the room into my lungs, and groaned backward with an effort akin to the final pushes of childbirth. His body rolled over as I released everything, ready to begin the next step instantly, but…

"NO!"

He was on top of me, and I could not move. Knowing there was no more time, some alien within me exploded with the force of an angry volcano. In one incomprehensible moment, I watched myself push 220 pounds of lead weight over to free myself. At the same moment, I flipped him again onto his back, this time without me underneath. Ignoring the voice that told me it was too late, that I had taken too long, I swept my finger into his mouth, wondering if he had choked on a peanut. He kept peanuts on the counter and would often peel and eat one as he passed through the kitchen. Sometimes, he would stand at the bar with a beer, watching a ball game and snacking on peanuts. He liked keeping the peanuts for the two gray squirrels who lived in the yard. They would often sit on the railing in wait for their daily treats.

After checking for obstructions, I started CPR. I never knew how long it took the paramedics to arrive on the scene, but I was told by a nurse that it took fifteen minutes. Being less than half Ben's weight put me at a disadvantage for providing adequate CPR for that long without rest. I stopped only when I felt my own heart about to explode from the effort, and then I resumed as quickly as I could. I watched as Ben's face changed from pink to blue, back to pink, and blue again.

"I can do this," I said over and over, to the beat of my hands on his heart.

My head was swirling further into the abyss. I could see nothing but his face, and I had to keep it pink. The words came out rhythmically as I pressed all my weight onto his chest over and over.

"I – CAN – DO – THIS. I – CAN – DO – THIS."

But I could not keep going. I stopped to take a breath, mustering all the power inside me to continue. He had stopped gasping and his face was blue. Emotion overtook me as I watched him fading away, leaving me.

"I love you, Ben. You have to stay for me and the boys. Please don't go. We need you!" I stroked his face, gasping for air, waiting until I could try again to beat his heart. "I love you, Precious. You're the best husband in the whole wide world, the world's best dad. I love you. Please. Please don't go." Blinded by overexertion and tears, I put my hands on his chest and pushed with my whole body. "I – CAN – DO – THIS," I told myself as I coaxed my spent body to bring the pink back. His tongue had swollen and protruded from his mouth. The terror of the situation loomed behind me, but I refused to let it overtake me. "I – CAN – DO – THIS," I gasped with each downward motion, feeling my own body about to collapse.

Finally, there was a brief knock, and the door from the garage opened. I stepped back as a team of paramedics swarmed around Ben and started working to save him. With my heart beating faster and harder than it ever had in my life, I pushed myself through the heavy bleakness to a standing position. Through a surreal whitewash of activity, questions floated around me, popping in my ears like kernels of gibberish over a blazing flame. "Medical history... allergies?" a voice trailed on. Questions about his full name and birthdate dangled in my vicinity, but I could not reach them or respond. Shock and horror had debilitated me.

"Let me write it down," I heard myself say over and over as I roamed around in a futile search for answers.

But I could not write or adequately answer their questions. I was in shock. The paramedics asked about what looked like hives all over Ben's body, which made me wonder if he had heat stroke or an allergic reaction to something. Confused, I took his container of medications from the kitchen cabinet and showed it to the paramedics. I saw that they had intubated him and prayed he would come back to us.

A female officer led me to the living room, sat me down, and asked me to tell her what had happened. I watched from some other world as my mouth responded to her muffled interrogation. My spirit was floating somewhere between life and death, chasing him.

"Come back to me!" I yelled through the deep, dark knowing that told me he would not.

I was supposed to believe that he could recover, that he *would* recover. I tried to hope, but hope evaded me. Instead, the heavy knowledge wrapped itself around me like a python, squeezing tighter and tighter until I could not breathe, could not think, could not see. My world went black like the formless void that existed before time began.

"His heart has been damaged beyond repair," the cardiologist told me two days later. "He had a widow-maker, a condition that often results in immediate death. Our examination and test results indicate he had a silent heart attack approximately three months ago, which significantly damaged and weakened his heart. When he exerted himself on his bicycle, it put a higher demand on his weakened heart, resulting in cardiac arrest. His heart stopped beating because it could not keep up with the demands of his body."

My stomach churned and rose into my throat as the doctor's words fell like lead onto the floor of the cold room where Ben lay with a machine forcing air into his lungs.

Did he let go because I did not believe? I wondered, despising myself for thinking I knew anything. *No! I did not make this happen! I could not! Please, God, bring him back. Tell him that I love him and want him more than anything in the world. Tell him that I tried with all my might to save him. Please!* Self-accusations clawed at me incessantly, ripping and tearing at the wounds of my loss over and over.

The next day, Ben's body could no longer maintain equilibrium, even with all the drugs and machines. It was time to say goodbye and take him off life support. With family surrounding him, all hoping for a miracle, the nurse removed the breathing tube. Everything was quiet. Ben was at peace. He wasn't coming back. I kissed his cheek and stroked the soft curls of his silver hair one last time before I said goodbye. But my tears waited; the sadness in my soul was too raw for company. In solitude, I cried loud rivers and held my empty body together as best I could, feeling as though my own soul had left with Ben.

CHAPTER 5

April 2015

I had not spoken with Simms since his dad's death because they put him on suicide watch after Ben's brothers went to the jail to tell Simms the news about his father in person. Simms was in solitary confinement, unable to receive calls or visits. I was a zombie, just going through the motions of what I had to do while also preparing for final exams. The thought of delaying completion of graduate school was unbearable, and quitting wasn't a consideration, either. I trudged onward, numb, as if the surrounding air was a clear gel buffering me from reality. Everything was surreal and distant. My hand was an apparition waving in front of me.

Was I a ghost? Was it me who had died? It would be a long time before I knew the answer to that question.

When I arrived at St. Andrew's Episcopal Church for Ben's memorial service, his brothers led me to a door where two guards stood, armed. My heart pounded.

Deep breath, I reminded myself, feeling something heavy sinking in my gut.

Simms sat in the center of the room in a fold-out chair with shackles on his hands and feet. I knelt on the floor in front of him and put my arms around him, burying my head against his chest so that I could feel the thumping of his heart over mine.

"I'm sorry, Mom," his voice cracked in a whisper. His head hung down over mine in the silence that followed. Several other guards stood as if they expected him to rip the chains off and run, or attack.

"I love you," I said, holding him as tightly as I could.

After a couple of minutes, the guards insisted I let go. I was escorted to a kitchen area in the back of the church, where I waited until it was time for the service to begin. Someone led me through a door near the front of the church. I watched from the depths of an abandoned well as my body went through the motions of convention. My muscles screamed with soreness, distracting me from the horror of my loss. The physical exertion of administering CPR for fifteen minutes to a man more than twice my size had taken a toll on my body like nothing else ever had. I welcomed the pain of each movement, clinging to the soreness as it suspended me in time and space like a paused movie.

Before the funeral, Rhett and I both had friends and family holding us up as we plodded through the moments in a dazed stupor. As a junior in high school, Rhett played lacrosse on his high school team. The coach and his teammates all tried to show support. When the funeral arrangements were confirmed, I gathered Rhett's dress clothes and tried to make sure everything was in order for the services.

While his father was in the hospital, I slept there and only went home to shower and check on things. The first time I went home, the day after Ben had collapsed, I found Rhett and his close friends all passed out, with marijuana and related paraphernalia scattered around the house. I exploded with fury, accusing him of disrespecting his father. In hindsight, I wish I had approached Rhett differently. He had his own demons to fight. Ben had recently confiscated Rhett's phone for some violation I can't remember, and I had given it back after his dad's collapse, thinking Rhett would respond to the situation responsibly. But when, in the fog of grave circumstances, he did not meet my expectations; I overreacted to Rhett's behavior.

But when Ben died, that world and everything in it was gone. Rhett and I were walking alone in a world where Simms was in jail and Ben was dead. It was just the two of us against a cold and bitter reality. Rhett and I were both in shock; coping with the demands of each day was like trying to keep melting ice cream on a cone. We curled into our separate lumps of grief and went through the motions like aliens on another planet.

Nevertheless, we both dressed up to honor his father when the day came to pay our last respects. Rhett looked handsome and proud in his dress clothes, and his presence beside me was a great comfort. We walked together across the front of the church, and my eyes glanced nervously over a crowd of attentive faces. The auditorium was full. Against the back wall, I saw Simms, still bound by shackles but dressed in the nice suit I had bought for his graduation two years before. I still do not know all that transpired behind the scenes so that he could be there, but I am grateful to Ben's brothers, their families, and everyone who made it possible. A team of police officers stood on both sides of Simms with guns and stern faces, casting a dark shadow over the room. The scene ensnared my heartstrings as grief began to coil around me and pull me into the depths of an icy abyss.

Without my best friend and soulmate, I was numb and lost. For the next several months, I went through the motions of life, completely unaware. It was as if my body was someone else's. Graduate school demanded much of my time and attention with a full-time internship at New Hanover County Regional Medical Center. It was traumatic to work in the same hospital where Ben had spent his last days, but I would not quit. Ben would not have wanted me to do that.

Meanwhile, Rhett went away for the summer with his

friend's family to play travel lacrosse. I ignored my grief as much as I could, as I imagine Rhett did too. But I found no escape from it at night. The pain ripped and tore and clawed me until my whole body burned. It sucked the breath from my lungs and squeezed my heart so tightly that I thought it might stop beating. But I kept putting one foot in front of the other, telling myself I could not grieve until my internship was over.

Finally, in August 2015, I finished my internships and only had two more classes to complete in the fall. Rhett was still traveling with his lacrosse team, so I booked a trip to California with plans to face my loss in the vast wilderness of Yosemite National Park. While there, I explored the glorious national forests of the Sierra Nevada and wrote my first memoir entitled *California Adventure*. Spending time in the wilderness alone allowed me to open my wounds and experience catharsis. As I drove up winding mountains and hiked desolate trails, I wrestled with God about my reality, hoping to find resolution. But deep inside, I knew it would be a long time before I found any—if ever. After two weeks of exploring, I bawled my eyes out before boarding a plane to go home. Little did I know, it would be four long years before I crossed over—into my "new normal."

CHAPTER 6

In the fall of 2015, I was wrapping up my last two courses of graduate school when the courts finally lowered Simms's bond from $125,000 to $5,000. My heart hammered fast and hot in my ears as I tried to absorb the attorney's words about the details of Simms's release.

He would have to wear an electronic monitor on his ankle and report to authorities regularly. I just wanted to hug my son, so everything else was glazed with a rosy hue through the lens of my grief and longing. I collected the required cash and went down to the county jail in a delirious state of hope, swirling with apprehension about what the reality might be. At this time, I was still unaware of Simms's addiction to heroin—and would remain unaware of it until after his release, when we could finally have a private discussion.

When I paid the bail and prepared to take Simms home, a technician outfitted him with an electronic monitoring device. It was a bulky box on a thick plastic strap secured so that it could not easily be removed. He was required to wear it at all times until his case was settled. The device was an additional source of stress upon his release because when it did not work properly, authorities would call me to find out where he was and why the signal was not clear.

It was a scary time for both Simms and me, as he was working odd jobs that changed locations. Additionally, these jobs required him to go into basements where the signal to his device might be interrupted. During these times, his cell signal would also be lost. When the monitoring company would call me, they would expect me to know his exact location and what he was doing. If things weren't resolved quickly, the terms were that he would go straight back to jail. Simms was terrified about this, and I mirrored his anxiety. He was trying to do right, but his past was already haunting him at the young age of nineteen.

Amid these stressful circumstances, I was buried in homework most of the time, determined to finish my master's degree, no matter the hell I was living in. Our daily existence was dicey at best with one main objective—surviving our grief. Rhett was not handling the loss of his father well, and he wouldn't let me into his world. He had compacted all of his pain into a cold, hard weapon against the world. His grief was rapidly morphing into anger and judgment toward me and others.

Rhett had turned seventeen a few months before Ben passed away. I knew it would be a long and difficult grieving process for us all, but I never imagined that Rhett might stall indefinitely at the gate of grief, refusing to pass through that treacherous domain, seeing no other course that could take him to life on the other side. I never imagined that he might not forgive me for surviving.

I found myself navigating an unfamiliar world cloaked in the blackness of a moonless night, a world bound tightly by the chains of addiction. The boys were both going their own way, and I had no idea how to make things better. Honestly, their strong wills and propensities for deviant behavior had taken a toll on the family even before Ben had passed away. So, with grief added into the recipe, we were all just trying to survive.

And although I wanted more than anything to show the boys love and support during this time, I disagreed with their lifestyle choices and couldn't seem to find an effective way of influencing them other than by attempting to do the next right thing each day.

Mostly, I did what I tend to do when things go haywire and focused on what I could control—myself. Night after night, I swam through rivers of gut-wrenching grief. And day after day, I ran from the horrible sadness, toward the goals I had set for my life, until exhaustion would come crashing over me like a tsunami. Beneath its wave, I would rest in my despondency until I could emerge with renewed vigor to run again. I could not directly motivate my sons or do the hard work of life for them, but I could model self-reliance, self-respect, and love. So, I did that as best I could.

Meanwhile, Simms was free and trying to manage his addiction. I still didn't understand much about it all—and with so much on my plate, including the huge loss of my husband, it would be a while before I did. Although I tried to act like a loving yet not overbearing mother to Simms, I didn't really know how to talk to him in depth about what was going on. I had become so used to him "not listening" to me that I had sort of given up on being the one to help him get his life back on track. I was just hoping he would want a better life for himself and find a way to have it. But I did not believe in my power to influence him. I just wanted to run away to the mountains and wait for the madness to pass.

Not long after his release on bond, I was cooking dinner one evening when I noticed his pupils were significantly dilated and his behavior was affected. I had been pretty good at noticing these changes in my sons over the years and had learned to trust my gut about them. I confronted Simms about his behavior and appearance and, admittedly, completely lost my temper. I lectured him about respecting his father's name, among many other things I don't fully remember. Then, with deep regret, I lashed out at him and accused him of breaking his father's heart —literally.

I was desperate to get through to Simms, and it felt like I had tried everything. I needed to get his attention. The fear of him returning to jail for an indefinite amount of time already lingered in the air daily. We didn't need risky behavior in the mix to make life that much more stressful.

"You *have* to straighten up, Simms. You've run out of rope," I said firmly, already devastated about indirectly blaming him for his father's death.

Over the next few weeks, things started disappearing. I wasn't sure whether it was the shady friends whom Rhett and Simms were bringing around or the boys themselves. I even thought it could have been my imagination. Was I losing it? Was I going absolutely nuts? I finally knew it wasn't my imagination when my laptop and TV both disappeared right out of my living room overnight—while I was sleeping in the next room!

Rhett slept a lot and showed many signs of substance abuse, though I will skip the details about that to respect his privacy. He was doing nothing at school and had been kicked off the lacrosse team, despite having been a star player the year before. The school tried to offer as much support as possible, but it seemed like nobody could really get through to Rhett. I knew his world had been shattered, but I couldn't put it back together for him— even though I wanted to.

Eventually, I found him unresponsive in his room one day and took him to the emergency room. I pleaded with him to tell the doctor he wanted help for substance abuse, but he denied that he had a problem and insisted he did not want help. The doctor said they could enroll Rhett in a program if he wanted help, but once again, I had to face the hard fact of love. We cannot live another person's life for them; we cannot face their hardships or pay for the consequences of their actions for them.

When Rhett refused to respect the rules of our house or even demonstrate basic respect for me and our home, I put my foot down.

"You cannot live here and mistreat me," I said. "Your father would not allow you to disrespect me this way. Either speak to me with respect or go live elsewhere."

After that, Rhett went to stay with a friend for a while, but he eventually came back home. I had meetings with the school because he wasn't showing up for class, but all I could tell them was that he would not listen to me and that it might do him good to repeat his senior year. However, the teachers and administration were determined to get him through the year and somehow pass him. They didn't believe holding him back was the answer. Rhett managed to complete his senior project on the topic of grief, and we all hoped it would help him work through his loss. Ultimately, it did not seem to have the desired effect.

On top of that, Simms couldn't leave Wilmington because of his situation with monitored release and a pending felony case. Rhett lashed out through name-calling, slander, intentional vandalism, and general disregard for the care of property. His actions astonished me, and I wish I didn't have to tell this part of the story.

Everyone makes mistakes, but these were more than mistakes; they were actions he chose. And every person on Earth is accountable for their actions—whether we like it or not. I have faced the consequences of my actions many times and recognize that I will always have to. I know I will face the consequences of telling this story—both positive and possibly negative. But I am not the creator of the spiritual laws of the universe; I only believe they are constant.

For this reason, I am telling our story considerately, understanding that everything does not need to be told. I try to imagine the best for both my sons. But to experience a life of joy and peace, we must all take personal responsibility for our actions.

I recognize that my decisions and actions affected my sons during this sensitive period of our lives—sometimes positively and sometimes negatively. For example, Rhett considered my interest in dating after Ben's death a betrayal. I tried to talk to him about it and consider his feelings in my approach, but he insisted on finding fault. Losing his father at such a critical time in his life was tragic, and imagining his pain over the loss has been excruciating.

On top of the heartache and challenges of the circumstances described thus far, my sons and I came into this season of grief battle scarred from years of dealing with family issues. One day, when Simms was about fourteen—or maybe fifteen—I found him convulsing on the floor of his bedroom with a can of compressed air used for cleaning computers. After the episode, I did some research and found out about huffing. Simms went on to try a lot of other experiments. Whatever he could find out about, he wanted to try firsthand, even though I warned him often about such activities and the permanent damage they could cause. It was like he could not hear me *at all!*

Meanwhile, I lived in a constant state of anxiety about whether he would live another day. Every morning, after the huffing episode, I was terrified to check on him in his room, afraid I might find him dead. This anxiety continued to haunt me, year after year, into the time of his monitored release—especially after I knew he was using drugs again.

Furthermore, after I had found Rhett unresponsive on his bed, the fear of losing my sons doubled. I was completely helpless, frustrated, devastated, and bewildered. I was like an animal being hunted by the demon of destruction, and my fight-or-flight instinct was turned up to a ten. All I could imagine was running away to hide until the horror was over.

I knew Rhett must hurt and figured the ordeals with Simms

through the years had taken an emotional toll on him, but all I could do was hope he would find the grit to push through it all into the daylight. I had given him the best life I could, with summer camps, sports, adventures, bedtime stories, vacations, and whatever else I could imagine might enhance his childhood and equip him to be a well-adjusted adult. But I couldn't protect him from the natural course of life, which put him in a family with our own set of problems—some of which I could not fix. Rhett would have to find his way, like all of us.

After I finished graduate school at the end of 2015, it felt like I was suffocating in Wilmington. Although we had had a beautiful life there, the streets, the restaurants, and even the grains of sand on the beach were all constant reminders of what I had lost and what I could still lose—my sons.

CHAPTER 7

One day, in April 2016, I packed my car and drove to western North Carolina in search of a new place to live. After traveling for three weeks, I found a town that seemed right and started making plans to move from Wilmington after Rhett finished high school.

Since Simms could not relocate because of the terms of his probation and Rhett did not want to leave Wilmington, I leased a condo for them and made sure they both had vehicles to drive so they could work, be together without having more responsibility than they could handle, and support each other through the next year of grief and—hopefully—growth. My role would be to visit every two to three months and stay in touch via calls and messages. In July 2016, the boys moved into the condo I had leased for a one-year term, and I moved west, to the foothills of North Carolina, to grow an organic garden, start an Airbnb business, and write a novel.

During this period of transition, Simms was on a journey toward recovery. The difference between him and Rhett was that Simms had started to respond to my concerns about his substance abuse. He expressed appreciation for the home I had provided to them in Wilmington and shared some details about how he was working toward recovery. His attitude toward me and my concerns was one of respect. Even though I didn't completely approve of his lifestyle, I could see and feel that he was trying to be grateful, responsible, and respectful.

"Yes, ma'am," he'd say when I reminded him to clean his toilet, throw trash in the garbage, and wash his dishes after cooking. And if he was trying to be compliant with my expectations by acting responsibly, I could work with that.

On the other hand, Rhett was still demonstrating a checked-out attitude. I made an appointment for him to see a counselor, which he agreed to attend, but when it came time for the second session, I couldn't reach him on his cell phone and he never showed up.

The counselor said the same thing I had heard from the doctor: "I can't help him if he doesn't want to participate in the process." What could I do? I couldn't make appointments if he wasn't going to show up for them. So, I gave up on that. He was going to have to find some sort of intrinsic motivation if anything was going to change in his life. It was devastating to accept that reality—just devastating.

A couple of months before the condo lease was up in the summer of 2017, I had to evict Rhett and ask Simms not to let him on the property. I could not bear the idea that Simms might end up back in jail because of Rhett's volatile behavior and risky activities. He had broken the fan in his room and shown general disregard for the property's upkeep.

Furthermore, Simms's case had been settled by then, and he was on probation. Rhett's attitude, behavior, and substance abuse activities were all putting Simms at risk since his probation officer came by regularly for visits and inspections of the premises. It was a difficult spot for Simms to be in because he loves Rhett and was always as tolerant and forgiving as anyone could be about their different lifestyles and opinions. I told them both that if Simms allowed Rhett on the property, I would have to make Simms move out also, hoping this would deter Rhett from pressuring Simms into letting him stay there when I was not in town.

By this time, Simms had found some stability with his addiction through the use of buprenorphine. However, it seemed like the criminal justice system stalked him, determined that he would ultimately serve his sentence. He was often pulled over, searched, and interrogated because of his criminal record. On top of that, he owed the county thousands of dollars for fines and charges related to his conviction and incarceration. Despite the demands of monthly payments to the courts, he managed to keep up with his probation and thwart noncompliance charges throughout 2017.

However, the threat of charges for not paying enough money each month was a relentless demon, continually casting a shadow over Simms. And it was not the only demon that lurked.

With a felony record, Simms's ability to integrate into regular society hung heavy, like dark storm clouds. And we never knew when the rain would pour down. Simms worked for himself as a broker. He would buy things from people who needed money fast and sell them later for profit. This was a risky business at times because of the clientele, but Simms needed to find his own path. It would never do for me to tell him how to live. After all, I knew what kind of blood was in his veins from his father—and from me. I supported him working, however that would look for him, as I'd long ago realized his life could not be conventional as a convicted felon. I believed he would have to figure out a creative way to make his life work.

The condo lease expired in July 2017, and I could not afford to keep up two residences indefinitely. I told both boys they would have to come live with me and abide by my rules or find their own place to live. Simms wasn't far enough along with his probation sentence to believe they would allow him to relocate, and Rhett wasn't talking to me. Simms rented a room from a long-time friend and managed to keep making progress. I kept hoping he could make it through his probation and move out of Wilmington, as it was not a good place for him to live under the radar. Eventually, he met a girl and started a relationship. They moved in together, but his girlfriend had her own problems with addiction.

In the fall of 2017, Rhett came to Morganton to stay with me. Even though he had not made the progress I had expected by that point, I wanted to extend some grace to him because the loss of his father was clearly still affecting him. However, despite my efforts to rebuild our relationship, his hostility toward me worsened.

"You won't finish it," Rhett said.

I looked into his eyes, searching for the boy I thought I knew, not breathing. The muscles of his jaw rose and fell rhythmically as his words sank into my gut, sharp and cold. My exhalation oozed heavily onto the floor and seeped through the crevices of the old wooden planks. His eyes shot daggers as he huffed into the chilly air between us. Pounding nausea surged hot in my chest, my ears, my throat.

I let the knife of his anger sear into my soul, felt it sink to the center of my heart and burn with the odor of confusion and sorrow. I turned without a word, believing that words could not penetrate the armor he wore.

Rhett tried to tear me down with his threat that I would not finish the book, but his words backfired as I harvested his rage to fuel my resolve. I envisioned the completed book in my hands and imagined my name on the cover. I saw the pages of my story turning, heard the whisper of its essence beckoning me—and I knew I would not stop until I held my book.

"I am coming," I said, pushing aside the ache in my gut, sucking air into my lungs, holding it there until it disappeared without release.

Then, I took one more breath... and one more, until I could feel love washing away the demon that tried to grip me.

After I had refused to be manipulated by his tantrums, Rhett moved out again. If he planned to stay in my house, I expected him to show me respect, maintain a good attitude, and earn his keep.

"If you want to be the head of a household, you'll need to get your own place because I am the head of this household," I said. "I will run it the way I see fit. You can respect that or move out."

He returned to Wilmington.

A week or two later, Rhett convinced Simms and his girlfriend to let him stay with them for a few days. Then, Simms went out of town for the weekend to see a friend. When he returned, he found his girlfriend and Rhett high on a cocktail of unknown drugs. He suspected they had used opioids intravenously, although Rhett denied it. Simms usually stays calm when things become precarious.

So, when he called and said, "Mom, it's bad. You need to come," I crumbled to the ground in the driveway, gripped by the vision and fear of losing my baby boy.

I found out later that Simms broke up with his girlfriend and packed all his stuff in his car as soon as he knew she had relapsed. He could not afford to stay there and risk violating his probation.

As soon as I had sufficiently composed myself following the initial shock of the news that Rhett was spiraling downward in what might be a deadly pit, I hastily packed a bag and drove straight to Wilmington. When I arrived, I called Simms, and we met at a local coffee shop. Simms pulled into a parking spot beside me shortly after I got there, and I saw him answer his phone as he was getting out of his car.

On the other end of the line, I heard a faint, frantic voice—a woman's voice—as Simms stood beside me, listening. She told Simms that Rhett was with her—and unresponsive. She believed that he needed naloxone, the drug that reverses an opioid overdose. My heart raced so quickly in my chest that one beat could no longer be distinguished from the next. I called 911 and explained the emergency as Simms told me the address where the paramedics needed to go.

A few minutes later, I pulled into the driveway where several emergency vehicles were parked, lights still flashing. When I went to the door, Rhett was conscious and told the paramedics not to let me in the house. He refused to go to the hospital or accept further treatment.

"I have to take your car," I told him from the open front door. "I love you, but I don't believe it's safe for you to be driving."

He refused to give me the keys, and the car mysteriously disappeared after I left. So, when I returned home, I hired a professional to repossess the car. Then, I flew to Wilmington and drove the vehicle to my house in the foothills. It was an unkempt sight to behold, and I took photographs to document its condition so I could explain it to Rhett later when he was sober.

There was no question in my mind I had done the right thing. Shortly after his father's death, Rhett had lost his first car due to irresponsibility. Not long after he got the car, he took it out one night and did doughnuts until the tires wore down to the tread wear lines. After some time had passed, I bought him a Jeep, believing he deserved another chance to prove himself responsible. After all, his father had countless stories of wrecked cars from his early years of driving. So, I expected some proverbial "bumps in the road" regarding young men and driving.

However, when I got the call that he had wrecked the Jeep, my concern about his driving increased—especially after having observed him at the scene. From my recollection, his speech was slurred and his eyelids were heavy. I suspected he was impaired, but the officer released him when he denied any use of medication or alcohol. Rhett had run off the road, barreling into a ditch and over the top of a sign embedded in a raised concrete block. The event had destroyed the undercarriage of his Jeep, totaling the vehicle. Rhett claimed someone had run him off the road, and I considered his story.

After a second hiatus from driving, I had bought a third vehicle for Rhett (the one I repossessed) and implored him to take care of it—which he did not do. For all these reasons, leaving him without a vehicle seemed like the most responsible thing to do until circumstances improved.

When I returned to Morganton, I called Simms to find out if he had found a new place to stay, and he assured me that he was fine. My mind was boggled about what to do next regarding Rhett. It was my opinion that he was in imminent danger because of substance abuse. I called Ben's brother, Rob, to tell him what was going on. The problem had worsened to a point where I didn't know my next move, but I was sure something had to be done. I couldn't let my son die, even if he wasn't acting like he wanted to live. Thankfully, Rob and his wife reached out to Rhett. After some coaxing from his Aunt Judy, he responded.

It was a delicate dance, but by Christmas of 2017, my in-laws had managed to persuade Rhett to go to Florida and stay with them for a while. I was relieved that he would be with family for Christmas and extremely thankful for their loving intervention.

I am free. I can make mistakes and accept or reject responsibility for them. I can fix what I have broken—or at least try. I can blame others for the condition of my life or claim my own power to change things. I am free to live and grow with gratitude. I can become resentful, or I can remain hopeful. I can let life happen to me and call myself a victim, or I can actively participate in life and determine that I will be victorious.

For many years, I fluttered around, trapped in a cage built by the ideas and opinions of others. I lived within the walls of convention, believing that to do otherwise was foolish. But one day, I found the door of my cage and pushed on it until it opened. My heart fluttered as I debated crossing the threshold. My gut told me that if I left my cage to dwell in the immense open space outside, my liberation would be final—for better or for worse. I knew I would have to trust myself out there, with no return to the legalistic notions of my past.

Nevertheless, I did it. I left my cozy cage without knowing where I would go. I stretched my wings and trusted the boundless power of love to carry me across the expanse of my dreams. Sometimes, the wind was so quiet, I wondered whether I was alone. But I couldn't go back to the cage, even though I was scared. I had to listen to my heart and go to my destiny—a place nobody else could find.

Though many years have passed, I still have to tell myself, almost every day, that I am not afraid. But I will not go back to live in that cage, for freedom finds true comfort in the cradle of a life well lived.

In the summer of 2016, after I had moved to western North Carolina, I needed to make some decisions about my future. Would I practice speech pathology, or would I set out to realize my wildest dreams? Since my undergraduate days in Houston, I had fostered the dream of writing and publishing a book. And with my mortality staring me hard in the face, I believed it was time for me to ante up. My spirit compelled me to break out of the system and live life on my terms. *Why not try to write a novel?* I thought and decided it might be the perfect challenge to distract me from the upsetting circumstances of my life.

As I began to research the topic, I learned that I would most likely have to write a bad story before I could write a good one, which took some of the pressure off regarding the outcome of my first attempt at such an exploit. I decided to use the goal of writing a novel as a target on a course of education and practice in novel-length, creative storytelling. This was my rationale, but it did not keep me from wanting to defy the odds and write an amazing story on my first attempt—nor did it keep the demons from haunting me about my deficiencies in this domain.

In addition to my autodidactic writing activities, I started a short-term rental business and a wellness consultation service to support my creative ventures. Although it was a frugal living, it felt good to be completely in charge of my own life. As a way to cope with grief and the challenging circumstances related to both my sons, I drafted my way through a couple of years. I couldn't live my sons' lives for them, but I could show them how to live passionately with grit, honesty, determination, and courage—or, at the very least, I could try. By the end of 2017, I had built a successful business, established a beautiful organic garden, written a relatively cohesive initial draft of a novel, and found a measure of joy in unexpected places.

CHAPTER 8

In December 2017, Simms was attacked and robbed by a gang. Ultimately, he was beaten up pretty badly and ended up with a serious concussion, which set him back on everything. His behavior and communication changed drastically after the injury, and I knew he needed time for his brain to heal. I questioned whether his behavior was related only to the concussion or whether he had also relapsed. I went to Wilmington and insisted that he come home with me to Morganton for a time of rest and recovery. It was evident, through his text correspondence and phone calls, that his cognition was affected by the concussion, drugs, or both.

Simms was determined to get through his probation so that he could move on with his life, but things were not going smoothly in that domain. He had a hard enough time avoiding trouble when he was healthy, especially after his conviction. Law enforcement kept a close watch on him. And with their constant scrutiny, I could see that Simms was at high risk of getting into more trouble, especially considering his propensity for deviance. I hoped that bringing him home with me would give him a chance to heal and recover from the downward spiral that was trying to swallow him.

After much effort meeting with the authorities and discussing the importance of Simms's relocation to be with family, we convinced officials in Burke County to accept Simms on their probationary caseload. Unfortunately, it didn't take long for Simms to attract negative attention from law enforcement in Burke County. And when a felon attracts attention from law enforcement, officers often find a way to charge him with something. Simms was charged with the possession of illegal drugs, which meant he had violated the terms of his probation. That gave Burke County officials the ammunition they needed to send Simms back to Wilmington.

I cried when he left, hearing the ominous whistle of a freight train. Simms's new charges were another mark against him as he went back to Wilmington, hoping to complete probation without further disruption. But, as a result of his criminal record, Simms was like chum to sharks, and local law enforcement was waging war on rampant illegal drug activity. I was worried because I had learned that even when Simms walked the line, his unconventional gait attracted the attention of authorities. His deferred sentence was calling like a ghost trapped in purgatory.

Late one night, I received an alarming call from Simms. His voice was slurred, and he wasn't making sense.

"Where are you?" I asked, trying to remain calm as I became aware that he might be hurt or in danger. I didn't know whether he had overdosed, wrecked the car, or been beaten up again. Whatever the case, something was wrong, and my son had called me for help.

So, I packed a bag and went straight to Wilmington, hoping things were not as bad as they had sounded on the phone. When I arrived, I tried to help him get organized and assured him that I was standing behind his valiant efforts to make a good life for himself. My heart hurt for him every day. Not only did I grieve for the loss of my husband, but I also grieved deeply for Simms's loss. No matter how much effort I put forth, I could not be a father to him. His pain was my pain. And it was a hot, deep, piercing pain that throbbed in my soul with every beat of my heart.

On May 3, 2018, Simms's girlfriend at the time called and told me Simms had been arrested and charged with opioid trafficking. Simms went through the familiar routine of saying the charges were all bogus and that he would be out as soon as an attorney could present the facts to a judge. Nevertheless, he remained in New Hanover County Jail until his case was settled seven months later.

I drove to Wilmington and visited him, but it was challenging because of the highly monitored conditions that prevented openness in our communication. We both knew that anything either of us said could be, and very likely would be, held against him in a court of law.

A few days after Simms's arrest in May 2018, Rob called from Florida. Based on Rhett's progress, including a steady job and regular participation in a religious-based recovery program, he suggested I drive Rhett's car down to Florida. It was time to give him another opportunity to steward a vehicle and move forward in his life with a new level of independence.

A couple of months after he got his car back, Rhett moved out of his aunt and uncle's house and rented his own place. Things seemed hopeful because he was working a good job and showing signs of independence.

But it was, unfortunately, short-lived.

May 8, 2018

Dear Ben,

I have your monogrammed handkerchief to comfort me as I sit at the coffee shop trying to make progress in my writing. I rock along this wavy sea of existence, soothed by the sounds of ordinary life lived by a beautiful array of extraordinary people. The fragrance of grilled bread and roasted coffee holds me in the present as the past tugs at my heart. My mind wanders to the time we took two-stepping lessons together. You were the most talented one in the class for identifying the exact opposite of the beat. Perhaps that was your predisposition toward jazz.

But let me change the subject and tell you about the boys. They are learning to be strong in your absence as they find your spirit in their hearts. I see you in their smiles, their walks, their words. Simms has let his curls grow down his back so that they look the way I imagined yours did in that picture of you with the ponytail, the front view where I can only imagine your hair falling down your back. Oh, your curls; how they moved me from day one—that day in Birraporetti's when you bought me a drink and invited me to your friend's backyard barbecue.

As I sit here in the coffee shop, I notice a couple across the room. The man's arms are crossed, his gaze distracted. His eyes dart around the room as the woman sitting with him speaks. She, on the other hand, leans toward him in an open gesture. With one elbow on the table, she leans her head on her hand to face him. They both have wedding rings and speak about a reception they will attend together. She tells him about the dress she plans to wear.

"That seems fancy," he says, leaning back to create space between them. "But wear whatever you want."

The woman offers justification for her choice and senses his lack of commitment to the conversation. She doesn't order a drink. Instead, she reaches for her water bottle with both hands in silent conclusion and departs. I feel relieved for her.

Later, when the waitress delivered the man's lunch order, he was cordial in words, but he did not make eye contact or show interest in her efforts at conversation either. I tried to determine what it was about his behavior or speech that suggested he was somewhere else. Another lady greeted him and offered congratulations. He warmed up to her by looking at her as she spoke and answering with some energy. But his brow remained furrowed throughout the lighter conversation that ensued between them.

Ultimately, I learned that he will be married in a week to the woman who left earlier. It makes sense, then, that he was on edge. I recognize that behavior now, remembering how you were all out of sorts before our wedding.

I miss your arms so much. Maybe the letters will help. Another familiar love song plays as I sit here writing. My glasses come in handy during these public emotional moments. A few tears escaped, but with a little blotting and breathing, I managed to gather my wits and continue writing without making a scene or running my mascara.

As I was saying, Simms has matured so much. I watch him walk, talk, smile, and speak. And I see your influence. I know you were concerned about him before you died. And if you were here, you would still have concerns. But I see his progress. And I have to believe it is enough to lead him toward a life of simple peace.

Recently, a tragic thing has occurred. Simms was charged with trafficking opiates. We both know that he has made mistakes in the past. And he paid a high price for those mistakes. These last few years, he has been making steady progress. We are hoping the charges will be dropped in a couple of days. He tried to relocate to Morganton, which we thought would help his recovery. The time he spent here in Morganton before they ordered his return to Wilmington was good. For one thing, it gave him time to heal from a concussion he suffered at the hands of a gang of hoodlums. You must be reminded of me in my younger years when you think of how trouble seems to chase that boy down.

Early in our relationship, you used to shake your head and say, "You bring it on yourself."

It's true that I had a lot of problems when we met, but I was trying to overcome them. I see this same effort in Simms now, which is why I believe in him, despite outward appearances. I pray that he will be free of these horrid charges.

Simms's girlfriend called today, but I don't trust her right now. I got the impression that her questions were baiting me to make incriminating statements against Simms. Maybe I am a little paranoid, but I kind of freaked out and set her straight about talking. Now is not the time to trust her.

I hope he finds someone he can trust, the way we trusted each other. For now, I will tell him to be cautious.

Love,

Champ (Cinnamin)

CHAPTER 9

May 18, 2018

Dear Simms,

If this letter finds you through postal means, it's because you are still incarcerated. If so, I imagine your spirits are low, and I hope this letter encourages you.

There is something I want to clear up on paper, even though I believe we have worked it out face-to-face already. That is the subject of your father's heart condition and the circumstances of his death. I look forward to writing to you about many lighter subjects. But first, this must be addressed.

You and I had a confrontation shortly after you were released from jail in 2015. Of course, we were both still hurting and grieving over the loss of your father. I don't remember my exact words, but I basically accused you of breaking your dad's heart, literally. And the moment I did that, I broke my own heart.

One thing I never wanted to do in life was say hurtful things that I could never take back. I have tried to avoid that, no matter how angry, hurt, or frustrated I become. However, on that occasion, not only was I hurting over your father, but I was also desperate to do anything I could to save you. Knowing I had tried all else, my desperation led me to try the only thing I could think of that I had not already tried. Nevertheless, will you forgive me?

I never blamed you for your father's death. For one thing, I have never seen much point in blaming. Blame tends to be destructive, and I prefer productive strategies. Furthermore, I believe that we all die when it is our time. There is nothing that can take us until it is our time, and nothing that can keep us here when it is our time. That is my opinion on the matter.

Of course, I believe in trying to save someone because we demonstrate love through actions. And our actions have an effect on others. And interdependence is an important dynamic of civilization. We all tried our best and loved each other. I am proud of us for that. One thing I know for certain: I love you immensely and immeasurably—now and forever.

Devotedly,
Mom

~

May 2018

Dear Simms,

Today, my heartstrings are tangled together like finely woven mesh, holding my heart like curdled milk in a cheesecloth. Just as whey is evidence of life in the cheese, my tears are jewels, glistening their statement that a person is here now, experiencing life in all its profound glory. I hold my eyes wide open and inhale deeply, recognizing the familiar heat and pressure of emotion trying to escape. I hold the air in my lungs and refuse to blink, but like a determined spring on the bank of a creek, my tears find their way down my cheeks again.

Over the past couple of years, I've studied what makes great writing. In doing so, I realize that I must stop scrounging around in my head for creative ideas. Instead, I must open my heart. I must write for love. This is what matters to me now.

As I sit writing in the coffee shop, music blends with sounds of coffee grinders and casual conversation. Emotion swells in my chest and my friends come calling—those wet, salty fairies that like to dance in my eyes and slide down my face, the ones I used to mistake for sorrow.

You've asked me to tell you more about my past. You want to know about your father's past too—and our life before you came along. My thoughts drift back to when I met your dad.

After high school, I hightailed it out of small-town Texas and headed to Houston to continue my formal education. My first year in the city was an education, all right, but most of it was about surviving in the city—not book learning. I rode the treacherous wave of freshman year and landed pretty low. I was broke and lost. I took a semester off to work full-time as I tried to get my bearings.

One Friday, after working my eight hours at Gold's Gym, I met up with a friend for happy hour at Birraporetti's restaurant and bar. We were sitting at a table in the bar area when two men came over and offered to buy our drinks. Your dad leaned over the table, extending his hand for an introduction. The music and conversation were loud when he said his name, so I leaned forward for clarification.

"I'm Ben," he said in a louder voice, "has been, coulda been, shoulda been, Ben."

I smiled and shook his hand with confident reception, enchanted by the spell of his wide blue eyes. They shone like newly discovered gems from beneath a mass of dark brown curls that threatened, at that very moment, to coil themselves around my naïve heart.

And eventually, that's exactly what happened. I fell hard. And so did he. It was like an invisible tether bound us together at that moment—a tether neither of us had any control over. And as the challenges of life fell before us on the road of time, we discovered that nothing could break the cord that held our hearts together. There were times we wanted to break it—times when we both wanted the freedom we had before we loved each other. But even though our bond was sometimes worn down to a thin thread, it never broke. And each time we mended it, our love became richer, stronger, and deeper than before.

What I had with your father taught me all I needed to know about life—that love is truly what matters most. I love you, Simms.

Sincerely,
Mom

~

June 13, 2018

Dear Simms,

So many things go on in my head. I guess we could all say that. For one, I've been racking my brain, trying to come up with what to do about you being locked up. It's heart-wrenching to feel your pain. I love you so much and want to do all I can to help. The biggest problem is feeling like the legal system is determined to get you. This idea clouds the potential of every desperate measure I consider for getting you out.

I've been plugging away at my writing on the novel—sometimes slowly but always surely. *East of Eden* is proving a remarkable read. It reminds me of *Shantaram* in its richness of literary genius. It takes such a special bit of prose to drive me forward in reading. Honestly, so many books bore me to tears. I have to dig and search in order to find something I cannot easily put down. This book is intriguing because every single sentence stands boldly on its own, powerful and compelling. I'm in awe of John Steinbeck's skill. It's incredible.

My thoughts about my own writing are that I have developed more confidence and ability in the creation of my own sentences. However, the weaving of an intricate story and the creation of subsequent details are monumental challenges for my brain. Nevertheless, I keep learning and writing, believing that my faithfulness to my vision will eventually take me across the finish line. I am determined to outlast any thought or power that threatens me. I will keep working toward my vision of publishing a book and allow myself to write about whatever I find in my heart rather than sticking only to my novel.

The distraction of your suffering and the absence of your father both affect me a great deal. I am relieved that Rhett is making progress right now—and that he is with family. Uncle Rob and Aunt Judy are very strict with him, but he is tolerating it so far. I am proud of you both for your courage. My heart aches and emotion wets my eyes at the thought of my two handsome Herring men chop, chop, chopping at life.

Love,
Mom

~

June 14, 2018
Dear Simms,

I have done some research about the legalities of your case. Here are some of my thoughts about it. Hopefully, your lawyer will know the laws relevant to your case and use them to your greatest advantage. We have to put our faith in him and the Almighty God. What we need is for your attorney to develop a genuine fondness for you. It is critical that he believes in your innocence. He has to buy the story you are telling to have the desire to fight for you. And in order for that to happen, he needs to trust you.

As you continue to work on building this relationship, I feel confident that he will make progress toward your ultimate freedom. We need his genius in that courtroom. And we have to believe we will get it. I plan to send him another letter thanking him for visiting you and working on every angle of your case.

Love,

Mom

~

July 7, 2018

Dear Mom (Mother Most Beloved),

Wanted to wish you a happy birthday. So sorry I couldn't be free to celebrate it with you, which has been the hardest thing to forgive myself for so far. I know you don't feel this way, but I know in my heart that you deserve more from me. With this in mind, I have decided to give you all I can while I am here. The only thing I can do to further regress the situation is to wallow in self-pity and dwell on the past—on what I have lost by coming here.

I firmly and solemnly resolve to make my time as physically, mentally, and spiritually productive as possible. I owe at least that much to you, and to myself. I hope that through my actions and growth, I can show you the sincere appreciation that I feel for the time, resources, and love you and Dad have invested— and continue to invest—in my life. I am left with no excuse for stagnation, having spent my life under the loving care and guidance of such exceptional examples of progressive acceptance and human growth.

I will forever be immeasurably grateful for the priceless gift of your love and care over the years. Oh, dear Mother, you are truly a gift in this world, directly from the hands of God. What you give, share, and teach in the world around you are immeasurable, unparalleled contributions. I have come to deeply cherish your presence in my life, and I don't know where I would be now without you. Today, I admire and respect you so much. I can say with full sincerity that there is no one in this world I hold in such high regard, no one I have ever held so much respect for, nor loved so much, and made me love life so much in turn. Your virtues speak through your actions. Your unmatched beauty inside and out is reflected in your youthful vigor. You are the embodiment of love—a beacon of hope to me and others in this world! You make me proud beyond words—thankful for where I have come from, proud of who I am, and excited for where I am going.

For all this, I can never show enough gratitude. Thank you for making me fall in love with life, Mom. Happy birthday to the best mother that ever was or ever will be! I love you more than words!

Your son,
Benjamin Simms Herring, Jr.

Undated
Dear Simms,

At various times since your incarceration, I have thought about how heart-wrenching it must have been to be in jail when your father died. He was relatively young and not apparently sick, so none of us expected to lose him when we did. You didn't get to say goodbye. You never even got to see him after your arrest. Since he did not visit you in jail, you were only able to make apologies through the letter you wrote him for his birthday. Thank goodness you sent that birthday letter!

Anyway, my pondering about you and your dad led me to think about the topic further. You asked me to share stories about my life with you, so I will tell you about when I lost my grandfather—the most significant man in my life, other than your father.

When I was six years old, we lived in an old shack called the Little House. It was a warm day, and I was swinging on a tire swing in front of the house when my mom came to the front door with a serious look on her face.

"Cinnamin, your granddaddy Long had a heart attack," she said. I stopped swinging and watched her face as she tried to hold it steady, lips trembling. "They took him to the hospital, but his heart was too far gone. He went to heaven this morning," she said in a shaky voice.

Her sadness shot right at my heart, doubling my pain. We both loved him immensely.

Later, I found out that my granddaddy had been in the hospital a couple of days before his death. I was angry that adults had made the choice not to tell me—not to let me see him while he was ill. He was the one I looked to as a father, and I was devastated to lose him. He was the man I admired and respected, the man who picked me up from kindergarten and took me fishing on the bridge. He was the one who taught me to hunt earthworms and tell the truth. I watched him go to church on Sundays with his gray suit and blue tie. I sat on his knee to the tune of "Giddy-Up, Horsey." He was my granddaddy, and I wanted him back! Over the next few years, I added gallons of salty water to the world, as I longed to be wrapped in the tenderness of his love.

It was the beginning of a lifelong lesson I would have to learn, along with everyone else on the planet. I get my own appointment with death, and I must face it with only God and my angels as company. Everyone else must stop at the gate, or well before, depending on their role in my life. Everyone in my life will have their own appointment as well. Through logic, I can see that some of those appointments will precede mine and some will follow. I must experience those relationships like waves on the ocean and appreciate their coming and going without trying to make them more or less than what they are.

Over the years, I've tried to work out how to handle all this loving and losing. My conclusion is that I must take off my shoes and let every toe feel the sand, the waves, the salt, the love, to take each moment into my lungs and feel everything that comes with it—the sun, the breeze, the cry of a gull, and the foam that marks my shins, clinging there when the wave has ebbed back into the sea.

It must ebb to flow again, I remind myself as I absorb the salty essence of the white foam and let its remains become part of the wave within me. My teary-eyed imagination gazes over the immensity of the ocean as salty air ebbs from my lungs and flows again so faithfully.

This is what I must do. I must honor the love I have experienced by allowing it to ebb and flow through me, like the unerring tide—each day, each moment, right now.

I love you like the tide—my precious son.

Devotedly,

Mom

CHAPTER 10

July 12, 2018

Dear Mom,

I'm terrified and disappointed about the loss of my possessions as a result of my incarceration. I guess my friend may have lost the money I left with her. And maybe she lost my other things too, like my leather jacket, my boots, and other sentimental items. I was angry at her, but now I realize that maybe she did the best she could. Maybe she is embarrassed by not being able to live up to my expectations regarding the legal situation. I thought I could trust her, and I was upset that she didn't help more. But now, I believe she did her best.

I don't want to resent her or be angry anymore. It does no good. It just hurts me, and I have done enough of that. I am trying to let all that go, trying to move forward toward thoughts about writing a book. I'm eager to get to a prison soon, as the county jail is wearing my patience thin. I'm hoping there will be some kind of relief with the change. I just have to believe something will be better there, tolerable. Mostly, I'm hoping to find some material for my book. Surely, I'll meet some interesting people there.

I've been working out as much as I can—a few hundred

push-ups per day and whatever else I can figure out to do in my cell. I got to see a dentist here. They were going to pull a tooth, but I talked them into fillings. They charged my canteen a bit for the work, but it was pretty cheap, I suppose.

On another note, I'd love to read a book or two written by narcotics officers, if you can find anything good. Murder mysteries and books by homicide detectives are everywhere, so I figure there must be a few good books about undercover narcotics officers, drug enforcement agents, or something like that. You always find the best books!

Thanks again for all the love and support. Promise, I'll make you proud. It really means the world to me. Remember when we were talking about people we do and don't want to be like? Well, there is no one in the world I want to be like more than you! You couldn't be a better mother. I hope I can make you as proud as you make me!

All my love,
Simms

At the time all this was happening, I was still working on writing a novel. Despite having studied the craft and worked diligently at developing myself as a professional writer, I was unsatisfied with the results of my novel-writing efforts. I could not get over the hump to take the plunge from drafting to serious revision. The story kept changing, and I found myself continually spiraling down a drain of self-doubt, frustration, fear, and distraction.

I wasn't giving up, but I decided to step away from everything and backpack through Europe for two months as a way of rounding out my education. That was my logical justification, but maybe I was just running again—from the pain in my heart related to my sons and the lingering devastation of Ben's absence in our family.

Before leaving on September 1, 2018, I made arrangements for one of my sisters to run my rental business and told Simms I would not be able to receive his calls due to international phone issues.

"It's okay, Mom. Do what you have to do. I'll be okay." I could hear someone in the background yelling. Then, some banging and chattering. "I'll just be here hoping for a verdict. Anything has to be better than this place—even prison!"

"I'm hoping too. You know I'll miss you like crazy, right?"

"Yeah, Mom. I know." There was more fumbling and knocking in the background. "I gotta go now. Love you, Mom!"

I gave myself permission to escape for a while, having encouraged Simms as much as I could. There was nothing more to do for him except wait for a verdict. And Rhett was still in Florida trying to find his way without my intervention. When I boarded the plane headed to Paris with only a backpack and no itinerary, I let my sorrows fall away into the broad blue ocean and thanked God for the opportunity before me.

From Paris, I took the trains around for a couple of months, staying mostly in hostels, ultimately visiting seven countries and more than sixty cities. And although it was a birthday gift to myself, my aim was to gain life experience that would help me as a writer. It was a difficult decision to go away where I would not be able to communicate with Simms during my absence, but I forced myself to do it, pushing past the feelings that I should stay for him. Intrinsically, I knew that in order to be there for him or anyone else, I had to be there for myself. To remain whole and healthy, I had to keep growing and moving on my own journey.

Simms understood. His support of me fueled my desire to be there for him in every way possible upon my return to the States. Maybe my trip was part of my becoming fully me as an autonomous adult. After all, I had met Simms's father when I was only eighteen years old. I needed to prove something to myself. And backpacking through Europe solo helped me do that.

Two months later, I flew out of Rome, feeling stronger and more resolved than ever to overcome my self-doubt and finish something. But my heart wasn't in finishing my novel because I was so affected by the turmoil of Simms's incarceration and Rhett's hostility. Each time I tried to work on my novel, my thoughts went to Simms and what I might do to alleviate some of his suffering, what I might do to change the direction of his life for the better.

Could I do anything to help? I wasn't sure, but I knew I had to try. The novel would always be there to go back to. But my son might not be. It was time to act in the present on something right before my eyes. These were the thoughts and feelings in my heart and soul—though my mind had not worked it all out yet. I was following a path of crumbs through the forest, trusting love to show me the way.

CHAPTER 11

Four days after my return to the States, on November 5, 2018, the courts found Simms guilty of possession of a Schedule II substance, which violated the terms of his probation. The conviction initiated a domino effect that brought down a slew of consequences, as his 2015 case had been settled with a suspended sentence. When they settled his original case in October 2016, Simms received probation (instead of prison) with the caveat that if he got into any other trouble with the law, he would serve prison time for all the crimes he had committed, including the big one—trafficking opiates. Ultimately, after the settlement of his 2018 case, the courts ordered Simms to serve a minimum of two years, eleven months and a maximum of four years, three months in medium custody prison.

After almost a month of waiting in New Hanover County Jail, the North Carolina Prison System opened its ravenous jaws and bit into Simms with a vengeance he could not have imagined. On November 30, 2018, he landed at Polk Correctional Institution, a processing center for new inmates. Not long after his arrival, he was approached by a gang of men who tried to extort him. The men told him that he had to pay them for protection or fight. Simms refused to pay the gang, and they subsequently jumped him. Simms's injuries were so severe, he was hospitalized. And when inmate fights require medical attention, the system makes a charge against those involved akin to fighting with a deadly weapon.

For this reason, Simms received an A-10 charge, which meant that his custody level would change from medium to close. This change would be devastating for Simms. He would have severely limited opportunities for education and rehabilitation. And worse than that, he would be housed with many violent criminals serving life terms for heinous crimes. Simms had entered a different world—a world where people saw what they wanted to see, ignored what they didn't want to see, and distorted the rules for whatever purposes they desired. There was no protection, in the conventional sense.

We were devastated, and all I could do was hope and pray for his survival. Once again, I was going through the motions of life with a huge chunk of pain in my heart for the three men I loved more than anything in the world. The people closest to my heart were either gone or hurting, and there seemed to be nothing I could do about it. How could I put my heart into a novel when it was broken into so many pieces? Although it seemed impossible, I could not give up on my dreams of writing and publishing a book. If for no other reason, I wanted to be a good role model for my sons. I had to show them how to stick with something to the end, even when it seems impossible—even when you think you are falling apart.

The day after I returned from Europe, Rhett called and asked to come home. I could tell he was in bad condition from our conversation on the phone. Apparently, his car had disappeared and he could not locate it. When I tried to make suggestions about finding the car, Rhett diverted the conversation to other things. Ultimately, the car never turned up, and Rhett never explained what had happened to it.

"Yes, of course you can come home," I told him, "but I'm going to run a tight ship."

"Yes, ma'am," he replied. "Thank you."

I picked him up the next night at the Greyhound bus station in Charlotte and took him straight to urgent care, at his request.

"I think I might be dying," he told me as I used my phone to search the area for a medical care facility.

After an examination, the doctor released him to go home, but he was severely emaciated. Out of respect for his privacy, I will not share the specific nature of his medical condition at the time. However, I believe it was obvious to anyone who saw him that he needed nutrition. So, I took him home and tried to allow him some time to recover from whatever hell he had been living in after moving out of his aunt and uncle's home in Florida.

Through the winter of 2018 and the spring of 2019, I nurtured my son and encouraged him to develop healthy habits. I caught a glimpse of the son I had not seen for a long time—the one I knew from before he had started using drugs. He even took initiative and applied for a college lacrosse scholarship in New York—which he received. In February 2019, he went to New York to further his education and play a sport he was passionate about. It seemed like things were going to be okay.

December 12, 2018

Dear Simms,

I waited to hear from you, missing you and hoping things were going as well as they could, despite your precarious circumstances. After a while, I determined that you must not be able to call or write to me right now, or else you would have done so. I made some calls and found out that I cannot visit until I submit an application and get approval. Only then can I schedule a visit. Additionally, the application is not available online. Inmates have to send the applications directly. I must wait.

On another topic, we got thirteen inches of snow recently, and it was beautiful. Wish you could have seen it. I will try to send you some pictures. Rhett is still here, but it looks like everything is clear for him to play lacrosse in New York. I was worried that it was some sort of scam at first. But after doing some research and learning more about the athletic scholarship process, I feel like we are taking appropriate measures to protect his interest while also taking the opportunity. He is looking forward to it, so I am happy for him.

I am looking forward to visiting you and learning about how you will be spending your time in Butner and where you will go from there. When I looked up your records online, I saw that you got into a fight. I'm hoping you didn't get hurt and wondering what type of weapon was involved.

Love and miss you infinitely!

Devotedly,

Mom

December 12, 2018

Dear Mom,

They took me to Polk Prison on the last day of November. I did not get off to a good start, to say the least. I miss county jail! As soon as I got here, I was approached by a gang and asked to sign a contract paying them $10 per week. I refused, but I wish I had just paid now. They jumped me shortly after I refused to pay. Police came and took me away—sent me to the hospital. Ended up with a broken nose, a shattered orbital socket, and a concussion.

What's worse, they put me in solitary confinement—and it's not like in jail. I haven't left this cell for seven days—no canteen, no shower, no change of clothes, and no calls! This is the worst thing that has EVER happened to me. I can't get the police to bring me anything I need. It took a week for me to get the stuff to write you this letter. I finally got it from a transgender guy down the hall.

I received an A-10 charge. Not sure how that works. But basically, it's for being in a fight that involves weapons or results in outside medical attention. I guess that also means I can't get home visits or work release while in prison. So, instead of getting minimum wage, I will make eleven cents per hour. And I might not get canteen or phone calls for six months. Not sure.

But that is all in what seems to be the distant future because it looks like I'll be spending two months in solitary! Can't get a radio. Plus, I'm stuck at Polk because they supposedly do not process or ship inmates during the Christmas holidays.

I hate writing to you with nothing but bad news and complaints, but I need to vent. I don't know what to do. Please write to me as much as you can while I'm in solitary because I feel like I am losing my mind. But please, don't write anything about God. I hate God. I need to hear from you and Rhett, though. It is horribly depressing being out of contact with y'all. I can't believe my pathetic life has come to this. I believe there is nowhere to go but up. But instead of going up, my life just doesn't go anywhere at all. It's dead. I'm dead inside as I lie here listening to the pounding of some heart nearby, thinking surely it's not mine. I feel dead, hopeless, alone, weak, ashamed, miserable, afraid, sick. I'm suffocating in the mire of my own disgusting vomit.

Please send books if you can because the police will not bring me any from the shelf. Even the guards that seem kind of nice just forget or don't care enough. Also, if you could check on my Burke County court date and let me know about it. I pray they send me to the county jail for that.

If you can send pictures with your letters, I think that would help me a lot too. As for books, I have some requests—*Burning Chrome* by William Gibson and a bunch of Lee Child books, except for *The Persuader, Make Me, The Enemy, Gone Tomorrow*, and *One Shot*. I have read those already. There is a book called *Treasure Hunter* by T.W. Something, and then history books on the Eastern Front of World War II. Hate to ask so much and give so little, but I need some help to get through this. I don't really know what else to say.

Thank you so much for everything, Mom. You and Rhett are all the good I have left in my life. I'm sorry I fucked up so badly. I had no right. Maybe if I hadn't been so stupid, Dad would still be here. Maybe I would have a degree and still be in school. Maybe one day I would be worth a shit.

When I did what I did, I didn't know what would happen. I didn't really understand. No one breaks it down for you and tells you it's better if you steal. No one says you can go to rehab if you steal, rob, cheat, or defraud people—but not if you sell drugs. Nothing prepared me for how traumatic it is to be locked up. Maybe I would have done things differently if I had known how being locked up would change me and make me scared to be myself ever again, scared to do anything because it might be wrong. Yet everything I do still seems to be wrong.

Who was that kid from high school who dreamed of being a doctor—the one who wasn't afraid to do or be anything he imagined? The one who was proud of himself? That was me, but now, he's gone—maybe forever. How could it not be forever? I've made an irreparable mess of my life. I want to believe there is some way to pick myself up out of this mess. I just can't see it. All I see is an endless expanse of black—no stars, no moon. There is only thick, deep, airless space—a hopeless void of nothingness. I race further into the depths of a black hole, further and further down, away from the light, away from freedom, away from joy, away from life. God help me. God help my family.

What was it all for? I feel like I lost the ability to look people in the eye after I went to jail for the first time. I could pretend to do it, but it wasn't real. I can't look at the people I admire as equals anymore. I hide inside while my eyes stare through a cataract of inferiority. The pure, clear look of integrity, pride, and confidence is gone—scoured away by youthful foolishness—scarred forever by the mistakes of a teenage boy. And that's all I have left—scarred eyes, shame, and a life of limitations.

I'm ruined. I am less than human, no matter what I ever do in the future to make up for my past. No matter how fast or far I run, my past will always follow me like a persistent shadow that cannot be evaded. When I stop, it will be there staring at me, reminding me I am worthless.

I imagine myself at a party with all those unscarred people, the ones with their right choices and prestigious positions—doctors, lawyers, businessmen, scientists, intellectuals, artists. Maybe if I get along okay and find a way to have some success despite my criminal record, I'll be welcome—tolerated. But I will still not be human. I will be like a monkey who learned some impressive tricks or a dog who gains notoriety for his part in a popular movie. I'll be a successful subspecies, at most, able to pay my way in, able to amuse the guests, but never accepted. The hope of belonging to a group I thought would be my peers is gone. At least, that's what it feels like right now.

What's the use if I can't be human? I traded my humanity for heroin—and heroin trades for keeps. "No backsies," it whispers with finality. "No backsies." And the cold, hard reality hits. I can never again be just another guy. What a sweet and simple dream it seems now—that thing I took for granted in my youth—to be just another guy.

I can't even get a legal pad to write on in here. I hate this state. I wish we had never come here. I miss you and my bro so much. It feels like life can't get any worse than this—even though I know it could, like if my arms and legs were gone, or my sight, or my mind. Yeah, I understand it can always get worse, but this feels that bad, like it's the worst thing I could ever bear without just dying.

I'm starving. Lost an easy twenty pounds since I arrived. I miss my cellmate, someone to talk to. Miss calling you. Miss my radio. Books. Most of all, I miss feeling like a person. I feel like getting past this and having a life is akin to being disabled and living with it—like it is something to overcome and live with, but it will always keep me from being what I could have been.

I'm sorry for being such a failure, Mom. I'm sorry for not setting a better example for Rhett, but I can't face the idea that it's all my fault. That's just too much to handle right now. I have to blame the world for doing something to me. I know I have to recognize my own responsibility in this, and I do. It's definitely not your fault—or Dad's. But the world did some of this to me. I'm trying. You know I am. But I hate who I am. But maybe that's only in here. Can't help it in here. There's nothing to love. I feel stupid. Love you so much, Mom. Thanks for listening.

Love,
Simms

CHAPTER 12

December 16, 2018

Dear Simms,

I got your first letter from prison on December 12. I remember the day because I went to the post office and mailed one to you on the same day. The mail carrier had not been around for a few days due to a big snowstorm. When I got home, postal deliveries had resumed, and the mail carrier brought a letter from you. A week before that, I received a package with the clothes you had on at the time of your arrest. Even though it had an address, I waited a few days to hear from you, thinking you would call with an update.

When you were in county jail, you told me you would go somewhere transitional for a couple of weeks. This is why I did not try to contact you sooner. I have been concerned about you every single day, wondering what to do. Eventually, I investigated the situation online and found out you had been in a fight involving a weapon. I called Polk Correctional Institute (the prison that had mailed your clothes to me), and they said you were in solitary. However, they did not tell me whether you were hurt.

Reading your letter was heart-wrenching. Your anguish

became mine—and what an ominous and terrible anguish. It devastates me to know of your suffering, but I want you to share all of it with me, because maybe that will help you. I want to know everything—not because it is pleasant, but because it is your life right now. And I care about you.

Since I received your letter, I have been crazy busy with work—repairs, decorating, cleaning, hosting, etc. All the while, you and your current situation have been on my mind. I have been feeling your hurt and wishing I could do more than send letters and books, wishing you were free. Despite hectic times with business, I sent in my application for visitation as soon as I received it. They said for me to call in a couple of weeks to see if it has been approved. Then, I can schedule a visit. Maybe you will be out of solitary by then so I can hug you.

At least solitary is giving your body a chance to heal from your injuries. Your letter said you had a shattered orbital socket, a broken nose, and a concussion. How long were you in the hospital? Was there a weapon involved? Try to include every detail of these events when you write to me. Describe your environment too. What is your sleeping area like? Your toilet? Do you have a blanket? What do you wear? Have you gotten a shower yet? Do you get a towel? Tell me about your meals too.

I included a list of all the books I ordered so you will know what to expect and when. I will try to send the lists each time so you can ask about specific items if you do not receive them. Additionally, I ordered the first series of Emerson essays. I hope they comfort you as they do me. Meemaw sends her love and prays for your deliverance.

As I reference your letter, I am drawn to the part where you say, "I'm sorry I fucked up so badly. I had no right. Maybe if I hadn't been so stupid, Dad would still be here, and I would have a degree, and still be in school. Maybe one day I would be worth a shit."

In response to that, I will first remind you that you wrote a letter to your father when you were in jail before. You sent it to him for his birthday, a month before he passed away. You apologized sincerely for the pain you had caused him. You told him how much you loved and admired him—and much more. You expressed to him your deepest desires to make him proud, to be the man he raised you to be. Since then, I have observed your diligent efforts to make him proud. I have seen you grow. I have watched you trying with all your heart to find your way among daunting challenges. In fact, some might even call these challenges insurmountable obstacles.

Your father forgave you. He loved you. He still loves you. It was hard for me to watch his sadness, hard to understand why he could not visit you. He wanted to get you out at all costs, literally. He could not bear the idea of your suffering, a fate he knew could easily have been his when he was your age.

"What could I have done?" and "What should I have done?" were the questions that haunted him, the weapons he used on himself. We both wondered how we could have done better. The shame of our flaws was a dark shadow over our home that winter. We struggled to cope, to forgive ourselves for our imperfections as parents.

I still wrestle with forgiving myself for not being perfect. But being angry at myself takes away the joy I could share with you boys and all the other people I encounter in the world. So, I have to keep finding a way to like myself each day. I have to accept and enjoy myself. After all, learning to love and accept myself teaches me how to love humanity. It teaches me how to love you!

Warmly,
Mom

~

December 2018
Dear Mom,

Thank you so much for sending the letter, the money, and the books! I sent you a letter and my clothes, but I used the wrong street number. So, maybe check around for them. Glad you took the initiative because I haven't been able to call or write. This place super sucks! When I finally got the books you sent, it was a huge morale boost. I've read them all twice!

They finally let me shower after about a week. So far, that's the only time I get to leave my cell. The worst part is that I have to shower with handcuffs, which gets pretty... interesting. We only get to shower once a week, on Saturdays.

I would love to have some pictures of you and the family, as I have none now. Maybe some from the beach, the mountains, the boat with Dad, and riding horses—just some ideas. You can also ask Dom if she has any to send.

Hopefully, I will be able to call in February. Right now, they won't let me get canteen, calls, or radio in the hole. Trying to keep my mind on brighter days to come, but this is a bad place. It makes me miss county jail, where I at least had a nice roommate, books, decent food, and my radio. If I can just get out of solitary, maybe I'll be all right. It feels like God hates me, like I've been marked. Now I honestly wish I had paid the gang the $10 per week. It would have been worth it just to be out there—out of solitary.

Send my love to everyone. Thank you so much for your support through this hell. It means the world. I will write again tomorrow, but I want to get this letter to you as soon as possible. Tell Rhett I love and miss him. You are the best, Mom!

Love,
Simms

~

As I continued writing to Simms, my heart and mind often wandered to Rhett, who was living with me at the time. Even though we were under the same roof, talking to him was difficult. I felt judged and resented, which made me reluctant to open up in person. So, I wrote this letter to both my sons.

December 2018

Dear Sons,

I got to thinking about blame and how all of us seem to try it out at some point. I guess it is just human nature. Some people start blaming and never stop. Seems to me those people are mostly unhappy. Think about it. If I blame somebody for my situation, I am saying they have power over me—power to mess up my life. They have the power to steal my joy. Do I blame others for the circumstances of my life because it is easier than making changes for myself? If so, I am not fooling my subconscious mind.

What it hears me say is, "Self, you are weak. You are a victim. Other people have the power to screw things up for you. Other people can do things to make your life miserable. They can take your joy. They can hurt you. They can take away your freedom to choose your own path and live your own life freely."

There came a point in my life when I decided, "Heck no! That is not going to be the way my story goes down. I am going to take charge of my life. I am going to be the boss of my life. I am going to chase down happiness and make it my slave. I am going to knit myself a cape of joy and wear it like Superwoman. Nobody is going to take it. And what's more, if somebody wants their own cape, I will try to show them how to make one."

I am not going to accept the idea that I am weak. Instead, I will try to be whole. I will recognize my body, mind, spirit, and soul. I will recognize the interdependence of humanity and nature. I will allow the power of my creator to dwell peacefully within me and around me. I will accept and forgive myself. I will open my heart to love and be loved, despite inevitable pain, despite my flaws and insecurities.

So, go out there and take charge of your life. Contemplate the actions and decisions of others all you want. Decide how you want to be like them or different from them. But never give them the reins to your life. Keep those firmly in your own grip.

Sometimes, the greatest peace comes from saying, "I was wrong. I do not want to be that way. I do not want to do those things anymore. I want to become better."

Decide what you want to become, how you want to be, and start fresh each day. Carry determination with you. Use it to get through each and every day. Never leave home without it. Let it be the blanket on your bed, the money in your wallet and the boots on your feet. Hold your head high. Smile. Be grateful. Be kind. Be in charge of your life and allow others to be in charge of theirs. Encourage others. Encourage yourself. Let the past decay to become the fertile soil of your future growth. Know that no one and nothing can hurt you without your permission. When you hurt, embrace the feelings with an understanding that you have a choice. Feel the hurt and let it fuel your dreams. Burn it for warmth and cherish the precious things that remain after all the impurities have burned away: cherish life, love, hope, grace, forgiveness, redemption, and peace.

With genuine love and affection,
Mom

PART II

Terms of the Universe

I cried at the revelation
As I gazed into the sea
That the only thing I'd never lose
Is what e'er becomes of me

'Twas a blow of immense proportion
As I stirred the embers hot
I'd have to learn to love myself
Whether I liked it or not

Of all the harsh realities
This one struck me most
Because I'd not invested there
In that wretched, haughty ghost

My recollection took me 'round
And showed me what I'd done
Endeavors toward faint sparks of light
Had turned me from the sun

When I looked again for truth
Through the lens of my despair
The Spirit waved its distant hope
I found no comfort there

And so, I cast off everything
Desperate to soothe my mood
I saw the sun shine brightly then
On a seed of gratitude

I took the tiny seed in hand
Then stored it in my heart
And within my despondent soul
'Twas a germination start

Despite my aimless wandering
The seedling fought for light
Its roots entangled 'round my soul
Through the long, lonely night

And lo, when morning lit the dawn
An eager sprout emerged
With open leaves, she smiled at me
Oh, how my soul was purged!

For from the little seedling
Reflecting bright and gay
She shared her love of warm sunshine
And chased away the gray

And once more, the air was crisp
My lungs were filled anew
The rain fell softly all around
And together there, we grew

CHAPTER 13

When we were all still in Wilmington, I had told both my sons I would invest as much in them as they would invest in themselves. After his traumatic transition from jail to prison, Simms showed increased interest and receptivity to my guidance. He also expressed a desire to help himself. Therefore, it was time for me to make my investment.

December 2018

Dear Simms,

I squeeze my throat in an effort to swallow the hot lump swelling there. My efforts only serve to infuriate its state, so I pull air in through my nose to cool the burning. My eyes blink away the tears that escape as I write on this Monday morning at the Grind Cafe. It rained all weekend, but today, the sun finally found its way into a clear blue sky. I am thankful for the sunshine and for some time to write between rental turnovers.

When I got the news about your transfer and the attack, I put my novel on the back burner for the sake of writing to you, knowing your agony is more than anything I can imagine—even given the fact that I have experienced a significant amount of agony in my own life. Ultimately, haven't we all? Even still, the physical and mental pain of your incarceration is something I don't even want to imagine. Nevertheless, my love for you takes my mind into that domain as my heart resides there with you, trying its best to wrap around you whatever comfort is possible —trusting there will be enough to sustain you.

The chatter in the coffee shop dies down slightly, and I hear a song from the mid-eighties—my high school days: "I Want to Know What Love Is" by Foreigner. I hold my eyes wide open and try to continue typing. The novel doesn't matter right now. It can wait. What matters now is this story—our story.

I have decided that I must listen to my heart. And when I listen, I hear you calling for me. I hear Rhett and your father. We are all in my heart together, doing our best to become all we were meant to be—bravely fighting the demons that oppose us. We are loving each other and loving humanity. We are leaving the past behind, living in the present with whatever joy we can find. We are learning to open our hearts so the light of truth can show us the way. I want you to know what love is. I want you to see my love for you and be comforted.

One day, I will hold you in my arms again, the way I did when you were just a little tike. I will feel your puffy curls and put my hands on your face. I will wipe the tears away from your eyes and kiss your forehead the way I did when I rocked you so long ago. One day, you will be free again. We have to believe that together.

You will run on the beach with the sun shining on your face. You will hike on a shady trail and feel a cool mountain breeze on your neck. You will look up at the great, big sky and see herds of white clouds grazing in their fields of blue happiness—FREE! Gratitude will embrace you. The fullness of life will wrap its voluptuous arms around you, suspending you in a moment of pure bliss.

Love,
Mom

December 2018

Dear Mom,

I want to write you another letter because the other one was so bad. I don't want to ruin your holidays just because I am miserable and you are the closest person to me. Guess it goes back to that old saying about how we always hurt the ones we love, but I needed to tell someone. Maybe pain shared is pain lessened.

Anyway, no progress. Still the same thing every day—three meals, four walls. Happy to hear that Rhett is doing well. And I'm sure I can too, when I make it out of prison. I know it's really only hard now because I'm in solitary. But they don't have cards or chess here at this youth prison because they cause fights. I can't wait to get back to the mountains and heal. I think I was really starting to heal when I went to jail this last time. I did some growing. I thought I grew in jail, but after all I've been through here so far, I realize I was wrong about that.

It's like when people think they are wise just because they are old. If I could just have some open space, some coffee, and a game or two of chess… I think getting out to Morganton with you really put me on the right track. Too bad it was a little late. I did some growing while Rhett and I lived together too. That was a great year! I guess the security of feeling like I had a home allowed me to grow because after I left there, things went downhill for me. Even when I lived with Jack, it didn't feel like home. And in the end, that strained our relationship. Glad I didn't ruin it.

Then, I thought I found that security with different girls, until it fell apart with Amber. That put me in the position to get robbed, which caused me great stress and depression so severe that I was arrested within days. Living with Lauren was great, until her sister compromised the security of that place. Even when it was good there, it wasn't all mine, which made a difference in my comfort level compared to when Rhett and I had our place together.

When you came to town to get me was when I really started to improve. Thank you so much for doing that. I will never forget that act of pure love, Mom. It means the world to me today—right now. But alas, the legal system already had its dark, parasitic claws sunk into me so deeply that it would not let go.

A vision of climbing Catawba Falls comes to me now. Remember when I brought Lauren and Rhett up there for Thanksgiving? That was one of the greatest trips of my life. I made new friends in new cities. And Lauren was a great sport climbing on that trail up to the falls. Then, on the last day there, when I dragged Rhett and Lauren to Asheville with no goal in mind, we had so much fun exploring the town, meeting people, immersing ourselves in the spirit of it all. That was a day and night that I will never forget—a time I will always cherish.

Driving through the city, I told Rhett and Lauren, "First, we need to find someone who looks like they are walking somewhere, ideally someone young like us, someone who looks like a hippie!"

Just as I finished saying it, Lauren said, "Someone like him?"

"Yes, exactly like him!" I said.

Then, we gave the guy a ride to pick up his computer. Next thing we knew, we were getting the full briefing from a born and raised native. We met his roommates and friends over the next couple of hours. After a trip to Black Mountain, they invited us to stay the night, but I politely declined in favor of more exploring.

After going downtown, I surprised Lauren, Rhett, and myself by running into someone I knew. I thought it had been a great day. And I was about ready to call it one. But Rhett's girlfriend had other plans. She invited us to a party and music show. Since it was our last day there, I rustled up my second wind, and the adventure continued. The party was not what I expected, but it was eventful. Shots were fired, people fought, and the cops came after we were gone.

Next, we went to Camp Lake James to swim and use the hot tub. It was one of the best days I ever had in my life—so full, so eventful, so stimulating. I felt fully alive that day. And I hope I can find a way to feel alive again. That's what I want. I want to get to the end of every single day and know for sure that I'm alive. I want to know that I've held life in my arms and twirled her around on the dance floor. I want to know I've kissed her passionately and tasted her bittersweet surprises. And when I lay my head down with the hope of a coming dawn, I want the day's reverberation to rock me through the night. Then, I want to wake up with the sun in my eyes, the wind in my hair, and dirt on my feet—the dark, rich kind from a deep-woods mountain trail. I want to hear the birds calling, and the water falling.

Tell Rhett I love and miss him, that I think about him every day. Merry Christmas to you both! Not sure how long I will be in the hole. So if you can send more books, I would appreciate it greatly. *A Song of Ice and Fire* by George Martin, *A Walk in the Woods* by Bill Bryson, or anything else similar to his book *A Short History of Nearly Everything*. Anything with science or history would be appreciated, but Bill Bryson's sense of humor is hard to beat! In fact, I'll even enjoy re-reading *A Short History of Nearly Everything* if you don't find something else along those lines. Oh, yeah! I almost forgot to ask for *Atlas Shrugged* by Ayn Rand. Gotta read that one! Hate to ask so much of you, but reading material is so valuable to me right now. I have read the first three books twice each!

As I continue to reflect on my life and consider what it all meant, I can't help but think fondly about my time with Misty.

The main reason I was so happy then was because I had my own place—a place I could call home—a place where nobody could tell me how to be. I was the man of the house, and I felt safe, like I was going to be okay.

I went to work every day doing what I loved—networking, brokering people for jobs, doing work that was in their field. I made friends all over and had a few dogs I was breeding. I had a car to drive and other ones that I was going to sell. It was nice to know I had a backup. Working for myself gave me such a sense of accomplishment and pride. I worked hard and was able to save my money since I was doing well with my Suboxone treatment. It felt good to know I could take off and go visit you, or go on a road trip if I wanted. During that time, I felt like I was beginning to learn more about myself, about who I was, and who I wanted to become.

Maybe I will get out of solitary soon and go on to adult camp. And maybe I will learn something about myself there too. Hopefully, they will have a good library. I'll have my radio. And maybe I can even play cards and chess there. Love you and Rhett so much. Thanks again for everything!

Love,
Simms

~

December 18, 2018
Dear Simms,

Today, I am thinking about you and some of the pets you've had over the years. You always gave your animals such fun names. There were the cats, Rags, Pancake, and Waffles. Then, there was Coconut, the teddy bear hamster. Remember how he got lost in the walls and survived for a week without food or water? He had found his way into that predicament by slipping through a door that led from your room into an adjoining attic storage space. One night, after almost a week of searching, to no avail, you heard something scratching in the wall.

"Mom! I think I found Coconut!" you yelled down with great excitement.

I ran upstairs with equal enthusiasm, considering we thought surely he was dead by then after a week with no sustenance. We followed the sound to the closet in your dad's office, and I sawed a hole in the sheetrock. Coconut came out looking like an old man hamster. All his black fur had turned gray, poor little guy. He was such a sweetheart—and a tough guy too! How many times did he tumble down the staircase in his little exercise ball? I think that hamster had a few extra lives!

The holidays will be very busy because I have a lot of bookings and turnovers with the short-term rental business. I am thankful for that, as I don't mind the work. However, it means I will be tired sometimes and may not be able to send a letter every day. You can know for sure that you are in my heart and thoughts every day, no matter what. And I will write to you as much as possible.

Before I go, I want to ask you a few questions. How are your injuries? Was your vision affected by the blow to your eye? What type of treatment did you receive in the hospital? Did they have to reset your nose? I understand that solitary confinement is difficult, but I am glad you are safe from being attacked so you can heal completely. I pray that you will find a way to live somewhat peacefully while you are incarcerated and that you will be transferred to a more suitable confinement. It is difficult to understand how the facility can let those types of injuries occur. Even more upsetting is they didn't contact me about your condition.

Has your weight stabilized? Did you get a shower and a change of clothes? How are you holding up emotionally? Tell me about a typical day. How are your hours in solitary spent? What do you think about? I know you will read a lot if you get the books. Write to me as much as you can and tell me everything. I'm so grateful that we can at least communicate through these letters. You are alive. You are my son. And I love you!

Today I called to ask if they received my application for visitation. They transferred me to the designated department and let it ring for a long time. Nobody answered. I hung up and called back to explain the situation, and the receptionist said she could transfer me again. I stayed on the line for about ten minutes straight. Nobody answered. I will keep calling. We will see each other soon.

All my love,
Mom

CHAPTER 14

December 26, 2018

Dear Simms,

I missed you on Christmas! I miss you every day. I got a second letter from you on Christmas Eve, which was really a nice surprise. Then, on Christmas Day, your old cellmate called. When I saw the number and waited to connect, I thought maybe it was you. My heart skipped, and I was flushed with anticipation about hearing your voice. Your friend was calling to check on you. I talked to him for a while and told him what I knew. He is hoping you get transferred soon and says he may be in county jail for another six months or so.

On Christmas Eve, I read the usual stories: "The Night Before Christmas," *The Nutcracker,* and *Christmas Every Day.* That one always gives me a good laugh! After story hour, we had a sing-along. First, I played the ukulele. Then, Rhett played guitar. We ate at Abele's Family Restaurant, which was warm and festive. Almost everything else was closed. Christmas was cold. I think they got snow higher up in the mountains, but there was none here.

I went to see my artist friends after Rhett and I opened gifts.

You remember Dennis and Margaret who came over for dinner one night when you were here?

All in all, it was a quiet Christmas, and my heart was missing a great big piece without you here. However, I am thankful you are alive and healing. I'm looking forward to seeing you as soon as my visitation application is approved.

Love,
Mom

~

December 27, 2018

Dear Mom,

It is almost midnight on December 27. They let me out of solitary today, and it is such a relief! The isolation here is about the same as in jail, but single-cell and smaller. I was never allowed to leave the room, but at least the food was a slight improvement over the county jail. They checked on me once every hour or so. But if there had been an urgent medical emergency, I would have died before they came around.

Population is a huge improvement over solitary confinement, that's for sure! The prison is enormous—like a big castle. There is a massive courtyard, but I haven't gone to exercise outside yet. I stay in a dorm with thirty people. The room is about the size of a volleyball court but two stories high. There is one television, one open bathroom, and three four-top tables. The kids fight a lot every day. They make weapons and really carry them around and stuff. The thirty-man pod has one phone, which the gangs control, but I will try to "rent" the phone to call you. There are eight thirty-man pods in one block, two blocks per building, and four buildings of dorms. We can buy sneakers, so I might get some after I get transferred to another facility because things get stolen a lot here.

Love,

Simms

~

December 28, 2018

Dear Simms,

Rain poured on the tin roof all night. It wasn't the usual thumping and pattering of raindrops. Instead, it sounded like the house had been relocated to the bottom of a waterfall. This morning, it was still coming down ferociously, and the yard had conceded to its new status as a series of small ponds. All the feral cats were under cover, and there was no drama under the house. Sometimes, Rhett and I hear running and hissing under there when they bump the wooden floors with excited activity. Today, everything is quiet except the torrential rain outside, an occasional rumbling in the sky, and the pitter-patter of little toddler feet upstairs. A couple from Japan are staying for a week with their young son. He wakes up before dawn each morning and raises all kinds of little-boy ruckus, reminding me of the days when you and Rhett were little rowdy tikes tumbling around the house.

I guess you've read by now that I got your letter and clothes. I know your attack was bad, but I suspect paying them would not have offered the ease it suggested. You would have paid for that decision as well. I wish you had not gotten attacked, but I hope you do not give in to those bullies. Of course, I might be wrong about it, but bad guys are bad whether you pay them or not. They cannot be trusted. I really hope you find a way to rise above them and stay safe without becoming indebted to them. I want you to be truly free when you do finally get out of prison.

You told me you finally got to take a shower. That is great news! I sent you some paper and envelopes with embossed postage. I hope they will let you have them. If not, I will order them and have them mailed directly from the post office. Perhaps that will work.

I have been busy with the short-term rentals and other business, trying to make sure money is coming in regularly. Rhett had to have his wisdom teeth out. Plus, he needed some clothes and food. We have been working on communication and doing pretty well at talking things through in a productive manner. That is good progress, considering the past year.

I am going to say goodbye for today so I can work on getting you some more pictures and figure out what the heck I'm doing next with my novel. So many things are swirling in my head. So much has been written, but I am compelled to prioritize my correspondence with you. Your incarceration has pulled my thoughts toward how I might encourage you and other families like us who are struggling with many similar concerns and circumstances. Perhaps I should be working on the book we talked about. What do you think? Should we work on our project as we correspond? Is it possible for you to write the things you think need to be written? Or would there be legal consequences for such open, honest expression? It just seems that if we could use our correspondence to create something positive and potentially helpful to others, it could be like a fire that warms and comforts us. It could give us hope for the future.

My son, you are not worthless. You are a human being. You are loved. You are valued. You have a purpose, a heart, an amazing mind, and a beautiful soul. You are a precious treasure. Nothing you have done can change that. We learn from our choices, and we forgive ourselves for the choices that do not coincide with our ideal. We let the past rot into fertile earth and use it for our growth. We accept redemption and allow ourselves to sprout in a new season, to grow stronger, to develop spiritual fruit we can share with humanity.

Look forward, my son. Open your beautiful mind and allow the light of truth to show you the way. See hope in the path before you. Fill your lantern with oil and follow her, one step at a time. The trees stand tall and strong beside the trail. Their formidable presence beckons you onward. They have survived the storms, the fires, the ice, the axe. Their vibrant green leaves rustle a song, beckoning you to some great and wonderful mystery just around the corner. You inhale the fresh fragrance of their life-giving expirations. I love you, Simms.

Warmly,
Mom

~

December 29, 2018

Dear Mom,

Happy birthday to me! Gonna say it's a good one so far. They took my radio privileges when I went to the hole (solitary confinement), but today, I managed to buy a used one. So, I get to use it before February! I'm listening to NPR in the dorm, doing as well as possible here.

The guy right next to me is from Motown! Small world, eh? He is a super cool, good all-around guy—one of those guys who doesn't deserve to be here, from what I can tell. He has lived in Boone and Marion, but his dad lives in Morganton. He is telling me about all kinds of cool stuff to do out there, like growing ginseng in the mountains. He says it sells for $300 per wet pound! Sounds like fun!

The dorm I'm in now is way better than the first one, partially because no one has tried to extort me in this one. The radio is a big part of the difference too; I love hearing the voices of people who are free and imagining that one day I might feel that again. Being out of solitary is a hundred times better than being in. Even county was better than solitary! And you know how bad things were in the county jail.

The TV stays on all day, but I'd rather play chess or cards, listen to the radio, or read. There is one homemade chess set and one deck of cards that someone smuggled in from county. Now, I also have a small window where I can look out and see trees and the sky.

Food is way cheaper here than county—like, fifty cents instead of a dollar twenty for a honey bun, and twenty cents instead of eighty for a pack of ramen noodles. Batteries are a tenth the price at twenty-six cents from two dollars and fifty cents in county! I haven't received any of the books you sent yet but hopefully soon. I'm really looking forward to the Treasure Hunter book. I heard an interview with the author on the radio, and he had some crazy stories!

On a different subject, I saw the psychiatrist, and she gave me Remeron. They don't give Seroquel here, but Remeron is a pretty good medicine. It's an antidepressant that also helps with sleep. I definitely feel better than I did. They feed us much better than they fed me in solitary, and we walk outside to get to the mess hall. I've done a ton of walking since I got out of solitary. The holidays and solitary both slowed me down on processing. Hopefully, I will be shipped out of here by mid-January.

There's a guy from Asheville here too. He talks like he loves the place. I really can't wait to get back to the mountains. Got a little mountain fever from talking to these guys.

"Someone" made molasses rum in solitary. "He" said it turned out excellent and was quite a treat. Thank you for writing so much—and for sending books and money. It means so much to me. And I really appreciate how much easier it makes my time. Tell Rhett to explore the woods and mountains so he can show me around when I get back.

Much love,
Simms

CHAPTER 15

December 31, 2018

Dear Simms,

As I was making coffee this morning, "Rikki-Tikki-Tavi" came to mind. I remember how you enjoyed that story as a young boy. That little mongoose was tough, just like you. He didn't give up. Will you remind me of what all happens in the story? I remember that he fights a snake, gets pretty beaten up, and is nurtured by a family of humans. However, I cannot remember many other details. It would be fun to read your version, so I'm not going to look it up right now.

Today is New Year's Eve. Yesterday, Rhett and I hiked to Harper Creek Falls in the Wilson's Creek Wilderness area. He wanted to climb some rocks, so I told him about the waterfall and the rope where we could climb up and down a smooth wall of limestone and into a ravine below the largest drop of the falls. He ran ahead on the trails and went off trail a bit, which concerned me. When I arrived at the waterfall, he wasn't there. I hoped he was not lost. Of course, he doesn't think that's something I should worry about. However, he had shed his jacket, and even his mid-layer before we separated, leaving all the snacks and warmth with me. If he got lost in that condition, it would be serious. But you boys seem to think you are invincible. Thankfully, I found him back down the trail a ways where he said he had stopped to wait for me.

"How did I miss you on the trail?" I asked him.

He said that maybe I passed by while he was climbing a tree. The air was full of a fine mist all along the trail, and the sounds of rushing water drove us onward. All ended well, with both of us climbing down into the falls successfully. The course down the slope was slippery with mud and moss, giving us both a nice sense of accomplishment for our efforts. Wish you could have been with us. Maybe we can go there when you get out.

I checked the mail earlier and found a letter from you. But I delayed opening it in order to write what I already had on my mind this morning. Now, I open it with eagerness, reluctance, and a knot in my gut—hanging on every word of the five pages you sent. After reading it, I'm frozen. Empathy curdles in my gut, and a tight lump that sits heavily in my core refuses to manifest in the usual ways of tears or tantrums. I run from it, staying busy with chores, eventually taming it with my steady breathing and gulping of water. Finally, I decide the feeling is hunger and ask Rhett if he wants to go eat. I still wonder what you eat there.

Love,
Mom

~

January 5, 2019

Yesterday, I called again to check on my application for visitation.

"The person you need to speak with is not here," a woman snapped at me. "You'll need to call back next week."

"I've been calling every day," I pleaded. "The person I'm

supposed to contact has never been available. Can you please help me find out something?"

The phone sighed and a softer voice said, "Hold on." After waiting a few hopeful minutes, the voice said, "We are short staffed. Let me check something else." My pulse raced as I waited. "Ma'am, the lady who processes applications comes in on weekends after her other job. Call back on Tuesday, and she should be available. That's our slowest day."

Disappointed, I thanked the lady, took a deep breath and held it for a moment, allowing it to gather the turmoil inside me. When I released the air from my lungs, I tried to let all the frustration go too.

I will keep calling, I told myself. *I will outlast their bullshit. I will be polite. I will stay calm. And I will keep asking until I get to see my son.*

Then, I called back the following Tuesday, and the person who processes applications was there.

"Oh, your application was approved," a voice said with a tone that indicated I should have already known—somehow.

I scheduled a visit for the earliest time available. I would finally get to see Simms for a contact visit! It would be our first physical contact visit since April 2018, before his arrest.

The first part of January, I had been working on repairs to the rental units. And as I worked, I thought about my sons and what my role should be at this point in their lives. I considered what their father would think and do about things and listened to my heart about what I needed to do. Each morning, when I sat down to write, my thoughts continued to land on Simms and how I might encourage him.

This is an opportunity, I thought. *If there is any chance for Simms to have a future, I need to find the strength required to invest in him. And there is a chance!*

This caused turmoil within me because I had set a clear goal to take my novel all the way to publication. But with Simms pleading for me to write as "as much as you can!" I began to see how to merge my goals and find peace without giving up my own dream of writing a book. For the time being, I knew two things: I wanted to write Simms as much as I could, and I could not concentrate on my novel. That story and those characters were strangers to me amid the drama of my life, and there was no room for them in my heart or mind at the time. I was a mother who saw what might be my last chance to help my son change the course of his life.

Would it work?

I knew there were no guarantees. But I also knew I had to do everything I could if I expected to find peace anywhere in my future.

My First Prison Visit

January 15, 2019

It was a cold, cloudy day, but the sun was trying to break through, making it not seem so gloomy. I was on my way to see Simms at Polk Correctional Institution—his first stop in the prison system. Google ratings for Polk Correctional are about the lowest they can get. Nevertheless, I tried to maintain a positive outlook, hoping I would have a good effect on the people I had to encounter in order to visit him.

Knowing my tendency toward emotional expression, I skipped applying mascara. As I sat eating blueberry pancakes in a small restaurant somewhere along the route, I was saddened to think about how long Simms might have to wait for a nice breakfast. Emotion stole my appetite, and I turned to writing for whatever consolation it could offer. I wondered how Simms would look. Would his injuries from the recent attack be completely healed? What would be the residual effect on his appearance? I was hoping that his sight was not negatively impacted by the blow to his eye socket.

My insides were a hurricane of anticipation and concern, and my whole body trembled as I walked to my car from Cracker Barrel Old Country Store in Burlington, North Carolina. In a sentimental fog, I pushed past my anxiety and drove onward until I reached Polk—a place more frigid than the mid-January day that surrounded me.

I turned left at the sign for Polk Correctional Institute and made my way toward the cinderblock monster as it crouched between the rolling hills of Butner. There was a circular drive in front of a single entry that made no efforts to announce itself, aside from a short walkway with a blue awning. A van parked in front was marked as inmate transportation. This made me wonder whether the door under the blue awning was a guest entrance or a place for inmates to enter and exit. The small entry building was separate from the main structure, and I noticed a spiral of barbed wire coiling the perimeter of the gray building like a sleeping dragon.

Polk Correctional Institute was lacking in street appeal, as you might imagine. The gray cinder blocks were stern and silent, shrouded by a thick morning fog. The parking lot was full close to the entrance, so I navigated back toward the outskirts and easily found a space. I was about thirty minutes late—even though I thought I had allowed plenty of time for the drive— because I stopped for breakfast and it took longer than expected. Maybe the real reason was my apprehension about the whole ordeal.

Not knowing anything about the visitation rules, I decided to try my luck at delivering an envelope of pictures, since they were allowable through mail. When I checked in at the window with my identification, the woman on duty told me to take everything except my ID and my car key back to my vehicle. I did as instructed and jogged back from the car, not wanting to miss any more visitation time.

First, I waited for entry into the small, guarded entrance building, which was connected to the main building by a sidewalk that passed through a gated courtyard. A heavy-set female attendant eyed me suspiciously and instructed me to wear my pass and go to the main building. There, another guard directed me to walk through a metal detector. Next, I turned 360 degrees on a designated mat. Finally, a female officer patted me down.

"Go through two sets of automatic doors," the guard said in a monotone voice that sounded mechanical.

The detached attitudes of the guards made me feel like a criminal. I felt a cry trying to squeeze its way out of my tightly closed throat. I held it down stubbornly with a deep breath and a forward march toward the menacing threshold.

The first door led me to a rectangular room about the size of two elevators put together. At the far end of the left wall was a metal door with a window. I looked with curiosity and excitement through the quarter-inch squares of wire that ran diagonally through the panes and saw inmates, all wearing beige pants and gray t-shirts, sitting at small square tables. I stood locked in the small corridor for a few seconds. Then, the door clicked as it unlocked. I took the cue and opened the door cautiously. As I entered the large, cold room full of prisoners, I looked around for instructions. There was a row of guards standing at attention across one wall of the room, and a few others circulated through the tables of seated prisoners and visitors.

A guard pointed at a table and asked who I was there to see.

"Benjamin Simms Herring, Jr.," I said firmly, ignoring the hot anxiety that was gripping and shaking me like an angry assailant.

For the next few minutes, I tried to steady my breath and

calm my trembling torso. Finally, I watched Simms step into the room through a back door and navigate the crowded room toward the table where I sat. His head bobbed beneath a mass of matted curls that swept his broad shoulders with each shift of his trunk. My heart quickened, and I flushed with warm emotion at the sight of my son dressed to match the other inmates—in a plain gray t-shirt and brown pants.

When he arrived at my table, we embraced for several minutes before the guards prompted us to sit down across from each other. My heart pounded wildly as I stared at the man who was once my baby, and I felt like he had come back from the dead. Gratitude contorted my face as mortality shone her aura, like a halo, over Simms. My heart was overwhelmed.

He could have died, but he is alive. I will not take this for granted, I thought.

And when I reached across the table to take his hands, the intensity of my feelings erupted. I looked down at the table and watched my tears land, in synchrony with the grateful whisper of my heart.

When I looked up, I saw Simms blink away the wetness from his own eyes as his cheeks rose to reveal a smile that had captured my heart more than two decades before—when he was my little Boom-Boom Man. The reality of our circumstances was a cloudy haze around us, but nothing could overtake the sun that shone between us as we took another step toward finding whatever good had survived among the thorns of our family tragedy.

January 17, 2019
Dear Simms,

Thank you for all you shared during our visit. I hope you understood what I meant about you smelling like your father. In hindsight, I thought about how it might have been a weird thing to say. He was the dearest and closest friend I ever had. As a result of that beautiful friendship, I have you and Rhett. For that, I am immensely grateful. When I hugged you, I felt a part of you that is connected to your father—the part that lives on through you. It was a beautiful, powerful, comforting thing. I am glad you have his strength, his beauty, and his intelligence as part of you. And I am glad you are uniquely and wonderfully made. My dear son, you are a treasure. I love you and cherish you from here to the end of eternity.

Today, I want to respond to something you mentioned in one of your previous letters. It came up in my mind, so I think I should write about it. You thanked me for coming to Wilmington to get you, for bringing you home to heal. You said you felt like you did not have a home. I can relate to that. I wonder if everyone feels that sense of lostness when they first set out to navigate the tumultuous sea of adulthood.

When I left Livingston at the age of seventeen to attend college in Houston, I felt disconnected and alone. I floated, rudderless, on a wonderful, terrifying sea of possibilities. Like you and so many others, I wanted the vastness of that awesome sea of possibilities. But no amount of wanting and understanding of the situation alleviated my apprehension. I hoped that time would. Instinctively, I knew I must cry the allotted number of tears, stumble the allotted number of times—and keep moving toward some mysterious destination in the future.

Eventually, I began to understand that my sense of belonging would not come from friends, jobs, a spouse, or accomplishments—not directly. Instead, I would find belonging in knowing and accepting myself within the context of life's circumstances. I would find belonging by learning to fit comfortably in my own skin.

Lao-Tzu says that "hope and fear are both phantoms," but I think hope is what happens when I see an array of colors in the sky and know that every rainbow throughout eternity is part of the one I see.

I ask myself, "Will I love, or will I hate? Will I live, or will I walk around dead in this body? Will I accept myself and others, or will I condemn us all?"

I want to live with love and believe in the beautiful moments that are scattered over the expanse of time, waiting for me to experience them.

Love,
Mom

~

January 22, 2019
Dear Simms,

The night before last, I dreamed about your father. I was at a beach when I looked up and saw your dad standing a few yards away. You and Rhett were somewhere in the periphery—all of us were joyful. After a few moments staring at your dad's jovial expressions as he walked along the beach, I realized I must be dreaming. Immediately, I ran to him and wrapped my arms around his middle. It felt so real! Then, I held my hands out, palms up, keeping a tight hold on your dad all the while. I looked at my hands and saw each finger clearly—five on each hand!

Remember when you and Rhett taught me how to have lucid dreams? You said I would know I was dreaming because I would have an unusual number of fingers—either too many or not enough. When I saw my hands with five fingers each and felt your dad's warm body against mine, it was as real as anything to me. Everything in my world was right for a few delicious moments.

In the same night, I had a dream about you. We were at a restaurant together, seated near a window in a front corner by the entrance. This dream was also vivid. You were in your Civil Air

Patrol uniform, and your hair was short, like when you were fourteen. Remember the picture I have of you and Rhett with Tucker on the front steps? You looked like that. We were sitting at a square, four-top table. I was seated opposite the entry to the café, and you were to my left with your back to a large window on a busy street where people were walking. There was a man sitting directly across from you. But aside from his presence, I don't know much else about him.

Shortly after the dream began, some authorities came to the table and arrested the man right on the spot. When they took him away, you broke down sobbing and I comforted you. The authorities said something related to the reason for his arrest, but I cannot recall what it was. It had something to do with you, having ensured that the man was there for them to take. You had lured him there so that he could be apprehended for some heinous crime. You had been hurt in some way by this man's horrible actions. Your intense emotion seemed to be the result of a huge burden being lifted and justice being served.

I don't know much about dream interpretation, but I enjoy documenting my dreams and analyzing them in my own way. Sometimes, I simply bask in the experience of them, especially when they bring me into a world with people I love, people I cannot be with when I am fully awake in the physical world. I am learning that my dream world is an important part of my own reality. It just happens when I am not obstructed by consciousness. It was nice to have the family together in my dreams.

Love,
Mom

CHAPTER 16

Once you are approved to visit an inmate in the North Carolina Prison System, you can visit them at any prison. However, each facility has unique requirements for scheduling visits. Simms went to Polk first because it's a processing facility. They send young male prisoners there for intake and evaluation before transferring them to a more permanent location.

When I called Polk to schedule my second visit, they told me Simms had been relocated to Alexander Correctional Institution in Taylorsville, North Carolina. I could drive there in less than an hour, which relieved some of my stress related to visiting him regularly while endeavoring to maintain my short-term rental business. However, his proximity to home did nothing to assuage the anxiety I had about how we would fill two hours of face-to-face time without the usual props like coffee, snacks, phones, pictures, or paper and pens for note-taking. But despite my apprehension, I plowed forward and scheduled our next visit for the earliest allowable date—January 26, 2019.

At that time, I had no idea how our visits would evolve. But I knew I wanted to love my son through authentic connection and encourage his development toward a more desirable future. Simms was also committed to our visits, and the hours flew by each time we met. I cannot even begin to tell you all we discussed in our visits, but we both wanted to make each one count. We agreed that the time we spent face-to-face sharing our joys and sorrows, and our dreams and fears, was the "good stuff."

~

February 2, 2019

Dear Simms,

I visited you again yesterday. After I was seated at table number seven, I watched for you through the door where the inmates came into the room. I could see the guard talking to someone. Something about the guard's communication told me there was a confrontation, albeit a small one, between him and one of the inmates. Then, I saw you peek around the corner. I waved, and the guard was appeased. Maybe he thought you were not supposed to be at visitation. I saw him holding a folded paper, one I guess he found on your person during the routine search before allowing you into the visitation room. It looked like he was lecturing you, or telling you something about the paper. If I were guessing, he was probably telling you to leave everything in your cell when you come to visitation.

Thankfully, you passed the screening and made your way to the table. I saw that something was different from last week. I felt it too. The brightness had gone from your eyes. They were not clear anymore. Was it sadness? Was it a result of the medication you're taking? I did not think so, because I think you have been on it since December. I know that the medication, mirtazapine, is known for causing significant somnolence. In fact, you said they prescribed it for that very reason—to help you sleep better.

I gave you a big, long hug, and you hugged me back. Sometimes, I wish we could just hug the whole time and not stop. Is that weird? Probably, so I stopped at what seemed like the appropriate amount of time. Just know that I did not want to stop. I wanted to keep hugging you because while I'm hugging you, everything is okay—you are okay. When I hug you, it's like a magic time machine. We are not in a prison visitation room. Instead, we are home, or on a trail, at a coffee shop, on a street—somewhere free, somewhere safe and happy. When I hug you, I try to take the pain away from you and fill those spaces with love and joy, hope and peace.

During our conversation, I asked you how you were doing. Last week, you mentioned how the food is a little better than it was in county.

"And there is a little more of it," you said.

I was relieved to learn that you might be better nourished than before. You also alluded to the prevalence of substance abuse within the prison system. Naturally, I am concerned about you regarding this topic. I can only imagine the humiliation of being in your position—the stress, the depression, the feelings of worthlessness that often result from such harsh conditions. I pray that you can find the best of yourself in there—that you can transcend your circumstances and find a way to thrive.

I love you, Benjamin Simms Herring, Jr. Stay strong, and remember to meditate every day. You are valuable. You are precious. You are MY SON, and you are one of the kindest, most interesting, loving, caring people I know. What you are doing right now is harder than most people can ever imagine. I know you will not let it break you. You will let it make you better. NO! You will not let it break you! You will demand that it makes you better. You will take all of it and transform it into something beautiful. Yes, that is what you will do.

Warm hugs and all my love,
Mom

~

March 5, 2019

Dear Simms,

It has been almost a month since I've written to you. I have seen you a couple of times, but that is different from when I write to you. When I write, I just have to follow my heart and trust that I am saying something worthwhile.

Speaking of writing, I have a lot on my mind today—a lot I want to write. There are many reasons I have not written to you lately. Other aspects of life have been consuming the time that I typically use on writing to you. Being able to visit you makes the need for writing less urgent too, I suppose. However, I do not want that to be the case. I want to continue writing to you regularly. That is my intention.

You could say I have been consumed with research, and that would be true. I am learning to listen when my mind tells me to leave things alone and let them marinate. I go ahead with whatever comes my way and wait for my brain to announce when it's time to write again. Today, I am torn because I have things to write related to the novel I was working on before you went back to jail. At first, I thought I would do that straight away. However, when I got to the coffee shop and set up my writing station at the small table near the bar, I looked out the windows at the cold streets and felt the warmth of my mug— smelled the comforting aroma of freshly ground coffee beans. The whine of a steel guitar fell on me from a speaker somewhere overhead, and I felt you here.

When I miss your calls, like I did this morning, it feels like I have let you down. I know you need to touch the world. And I am your eyes, your ears, your hands, and your feet out here—for now. I am glad that you have connected with some friends on the outside too, but I know that is different. Honestly, I feel a bit weepy for missing your call because I did not get to see you this past weekend. We decided to change our visits to every other week. It seemed reasonable to both of us. I cried during our last visit, and I know that is hard for you.

As I sit here holding back the tears, I think about a blueberry muffin and want to eat one for comfort. Maybe I will. The old-time country music they play here at the Grind Cafe on Tuesdays takes me back to my childhood and suspends me there with the weight of that time and the weight of this one—all mixed together.

When I really consider what is going on, I suppose I am grieving for you. I am hurting for you and wishing I could have done something better. I read a book yesterday entitled *The Silent Patient*. The author commented on Freud as he wove a complex psychological tale. He wrote about how when we are in the womb—and when we are infants—we are affected by our parents' emotional states.

"Will you please heat my coffee for a minute or two?" I paused my writing to ask the barista.

"Of course!" she said with a warm smile as she reached for my mug and swept it across the counter with a graceful twirl.

I went to the bathroom for a brief cry, dried my tears, and returned to the counter to pick up my warm coffee and admire the blueberry muffin again. *I will have a salad later,* I thought to myself, wondering how resolved I was toward that aim. With a sip of my rejuvenated joe, I got back on track and continued writing.

The author of the novel commented on the effects of our emotions on an unborn infant—and beyond that, into early childhood. When I became pregnant with you, I was determined to overcome everything from my past. Determined to give my baby the best chance in life, I read all the latest books on pregnancy and parenting. Having finished college and taught for a couple of years, I thought the timing was right.

After you were born, your father came to pick us up from the hospital, and the nurses rolled me to the elevator. I held you close until we reached the vehicle. A nurse took you and placed you in the car seat. My body trembled all over as I struggled to buckle you in. Emotion overcame me, and I cried. Alarmed nurses questioned me, concerned that I might have postpartum depression. I assured them I was okay—that the reason for my lability was love and an intense recognition of responsibility to this tiny, vulnerable, precious little being. I was terrified to my very core that I could not be good enough. At that moment, I hoped and prayed I could do right by you.

Knowing I was responsible for keeping a fragile little human alive scared me like nothing else in the world has ever scared me. I prayed with everything inside me, pleading with God for help, knowing it would take a miracle. Surely, you felt my love, but maybe you also felt the other things. Through all the things I did right, all I could see were the things I did wrong.

Despite my feelings of inadequacy, I did everything in my power—and asked for God's supernatural power—every day. I wanted to be a relaxed mother, but I wasn't—not for a while. I worried about doing everything right. You did not drink enough milk, according to the doctors. You were underweight. It seemed like I was failing, despite my best efforts. Everyone had an opinion, and I found myself believing that all of those opinions must be better than my own.

Looking back on it, I was an emotional mess. Admittedly, I turned to marijuana at times for its calming effect. I had given it up before becoming pregnant with you and did not smoke during the pregnancy because I wanted to give you the best chance at everything. I knew I could never forgive myself if I put you at risk and something went wrong. The pregnancy was a good one, and you moved a lot. I enjoyed that time—having you so close to me. I was excited to know you. I read to you, sang to you, rocked with you, and worked in my classroom a lot.

At that time, I was teaching second grade at Housman Elementary in Houston, Texas. I approached my teaching job as fervently as I did everything else, wanting to be the best teacher possible. I worked long hours and obsessed over every detail of my classroom—every lesson, every student. I believed in doing whatever I did with excellence. I guess I hoped I could find peace in my efforts to steward all of my abilities by using them with passionate enthusiasm. When sadness and anxiety haunted me, I would at least have an argument. I could rebut those negative messages with solid facts. I could give examples of how I had done my very best at this and that—and something else. It was like dousing hot coals with sprinkles of water. It kept them from charring the meat, but the coals did not stop burning, heating, haunting. The demons of my past looked for cracks like mice in an old house. They were determined to find ways out, no matter how diligent I was at patching holes. Apparently, they were agile and persistent, bred to survive generation after generation.

Even though I often felt these demons trying to overpower me, I had to believe there was a way to defeat the cycle of oppression. But grace was a distant apparition most of the time evading the space around my present hour. She was out of reach —in the shadows. She stood where I could see her with an expression of compassion. Her eyes looked at me with longing, as if she wondered why I would not allow her close to me. She was willing to be there, but something was between us, something I knew I had to get past.

But what was it? How would I defeat it? How could I defeat an obstacle I could not see—or even begin to identify? After all, I had confronted the demons I knew. I had told the truth about what happened to me and suffered the repercussions. I had cried and soothed myself with alcohol and marijuana, and occasionally other experiments. All of it left me feeling more bewildered, more lost, further from where I wanted to go.

And... I ate the blueberry muffin. The top was golden brown and gooey soft. It tasted like the doughy brown surface on a perfectly baked white wedding cake. Granny Long, my father's mother, used to bake cakes professionally. She would carefully scrape the golden dough off the warm cake before icing it and give it to me on a small saucer. I would roll the prize into small golden balls of warm, soft sweetness and let them melt in my mouth one after the other. It was like a portal to heaven. Surely, when God said the streets of heaven were paved with gold, he meant that gold—the warm, sweet, delicious, doughy gold from Granny's oven. Yes, that was heaven, melting in my mouth and sliding into my stomach as it told me that everything in the world was all right.

That heavenly experience was a refuge too, while it lasted. But those years came to an end, and my next heaven was in a swirly glass pipe on the back porch. During the day, I would attend to all my responsibilities diligently with the goal of doing everything right. I would wear myself completely out to earn my nights' relief. When all was said and done at work, and you were snuggly asleep in your bed, I would find my reward in a fragrant little green cannabis bud.

It's not that bad, I had told myself. The problem is that anything can be compared to something worse. I knew the truth. Lungs need fresh air. Smoke is not ideal for lungs. In fact, smoke hurts lungs. It burns and leaves carcinogens behind. But I lied to myself about this, or just neglected the subject. After all, I deserved to feel good, right? It was my reward for working hard and being a good girl all day. I did everything I thought everyone else needed. I deserved to feel okay for a little while. I knew it was a lie, but it was what I wanted at the time. It was what I thought I needed.

Funny how humans tend to reward ourselves with things that are bad for us. We poison ourselves with alcohol, sugar, smoke, or some other out-of-balance habit that wears away at us, dulling our pain by dulling our sense of being alive. As we kill ourselves, we dull the pain and make ourselves numb to everything in life. Our experience becomes something out in the distance that we watch like it's on a TV screen. We don't feel it; we just watch it happen until everything goes black and someone pronounces that we have, in fact, died.

As the years ticked by, I knew my grace period (that time of youth when one's body is more resilient to abuse) would run out. I had to find a way to appreciate life without letting it destroy me. I decided to wake up every day and thank God for giving me all I need. One day at a time, I practiced seeing good things and thanking God for all the wonder in the world. And over the years, I came to recognize what once was sadness as gratitude.

Now, when I feel emotional because of someone else's plight, or because of my own, I breathe in air and imagine the release of anxiety with each exhale. I am grateful. The air fills my lungs, the water fills my belly, the ground holds me. I am okay. I am safe. I am alive. I feel the sadness, the joy, the pain, the excitement, the hope—and most of all, the love. Sometimes, these feelings are so intense that it overwhelms me. I am tempted to mute them. Then, I remember that if my feelings are muted, I am dead. This thought transforms my perspective, and I allow the tumultuous sea of emotions within me to flow toward life. I let my emotions bloom. They are the flower of my being—a deeply precious and unique manifestation that reveals the complexities of my soul.

I can feel, and so I am alive. Thank God, I am alive.

With much love,

Mom

CHAPTER 17

March 13, 2019

Dear Simms,

I saw you on March 9, the day after your dad's birthday. We had a good visit, although it was a short one. Between a change in the visitation schedule and urgent demands with the short-term rental, I arrived late for the visit. But we made the best of the hour we had.

You emerged with a spring in your step and a smile on your beautiful face. With relaxed gestures and a steady gaze, you told me about small changes that have made a big difference in your incarceration experience.

"I'm on the fourth floor now, so I can get a radio signal most of the time," you said. "And my window doesn't fog up, so I can see outside! The window isn't very wide, just a couple of inches, but I can see a dirt trail and some grass," you went on, shifting your weight and leaning forward in your chair with a big smile. "The inmates and guards are a little more chill in this block, so sometimes, it feels almost normal."

My heart swelled with joy at the sight of you feeling good for a change.

At the end of our visit, you confessed that you were purposefully displaying a more positive attitude during our visit out of consideration for me. You said that in a conversation with a cellmate, he reminded you that your loved ones are doing this time with you. He mentioned how it is hard for us too. Of course, you knew this, but the reminder prompted you to contemplate it. I appreciate your genuine efforts to alleviate some of my burden. It was truly encouraging to see your smile and feel your spirit vibrate at a higher frequency. Thank you for that. Ultimately, I want you to share authentically and allow me to take some of the burden too. It is my desire to encourage you and be a positive and supportive force in your life through these circumstances and into the future. I love you. You are a priceless treasure.

It's Wednesday, and I'm finally getting some writing time at Grind Cafe. The early part of the week was busy with turning over the rental units and visiting your meemaw. After that, I had to dig through storage to find some things for Rhett. Another thing that added to my schedule happened on my way back from seeing you. One of my tires was low on air, so I stopped to put some in. While I was inside the store getting quarters for the air machine, an elderly lady backed into my car. Thankfully, she didn't drive away, so her insurance is covering the damage. I had to get an estimate and take care of all that. So, life keeps handing me things to do, and I keep plugging away. Finally, things settled down today, and I am so happy to be writing. I miss it a lot when I cannot do so. Things tumble around in my head, begging to be written, organized, worked out.

One thing that's been tumbling around relates to our most recent visit. As I reflected on our conversation, I realized that I got off on a few lengthy tangents and did not maintain a proper balance of exchange. It bothers me because I want to be a better listener. I want to know you better by hearing what you think and learning what is important to you.

You are a good listener, and I admire that about you. Thank you for listening so sincerely when I talk to you. It makes me feel valued and loved. You have such a beautiful soul, my dear son. I love you more than words can express. Nevertheless, I will keep putting one word after another toward that aim and hope that some of them are effective in expressing the depth of my endearment.

Your friend, Mike, who has been writing to you during your incarceration, has been doing some research related to correspondence courses. I wonder if this is something you really want to do. You are such an avid and enthusiastic learner. If you ever decide you want to earn a degree, or get more formal education, I will support those endeavors one hundred percent. But the first thing you must decide is who you are doing it for. The only way it will be worth it is if you do it for YOURSELF— not for a friend, not for me, not for Rhett—but for YOURSELF. That being said, I will do all I can to support and encourage your personal educational pursuits.

All my love,
Mom

~

Early April 2019
Dear Mom,

I wasn't going to send a letter yet, but I figure you deserve one. So, yeah, I got moved back to my old block, but I had been doing well in the school block. I had a few chess players there and a couple of guys with shared interests and a sense of humor. Also, I just found out that there are "no jobs available." WTF?! So, I'm having a rough time currently. My ceiling leaks water onto my bed constantly, driving me INSANE from the dripping noise while making my bed and pillow soaking wet!

Mostly, I try to keep coping with the overwhelming despair and crippling depression on a daily basis. Coffee helps some— and the meds I get. But the system is set up where treatment is inflexible. I can't just try something new, or adjust meds regularly. Plus, there are many meds they refuse to give because people seek them out and willfully take them. For this reason, they consider them abused—even though they have no recreational value. Why can't they understand that people seek them because they are effective medications for management of symptoms?

I've had no outside time or library since I moved blocks. So, I have been in a rut, not listening to the radio except for news. I still have enough to read, but I'm trying to keep myself motivated to read—at least if I am not going to write. It's hard to accept my vision starting to go bad on me. It's always been so excellent. Suddenly, I feel like I am getting old—or dying, is more like it. I have been gaining weight steadily, probably mostly because of the meds I'm on, as they are all bad weight-gain meds. When I don't take them, my appetite disappears. I am 210 pounds now and feel what it must be like to not be able to control weight, as I've watched myself steadily creep up from 190.

When I was at Central Prison, a nurse said something that scared the shit out of me. She was going through my medical history and said I had a history of hepatitis. I was tested in jail and didn't get the results back, which was supposed to mean I was clean. I am hoping that someone just misheard me during a physical or something, but I have been scared to get retested. They have a cure for hep C now, and it's super common— especially in jails and prisons where hep C is an epidemic. Cure or not, it has troubled me nonstop since. I may have been clean before jail and contracted it there, or in prison, since they took blood in processing. So, feeling pretty bleak, like my body is giving up on me. Doing my best to keep my head up for you and Rhett. Love you more than anything in the world.

Love,

Simms

P.S. I feel a little better after writing this.

CHAPTER 18

April 14, 2019

I visited Simms yesterday, and we were both a little sleepy. As we conversed, I noticed how our conversation reflected the drowsy mood we both brought to the table. During our visits, we must sit facing each other at a table with our hands visible. No devices are allowed. In fact, nothing is allowed, except my car key and driver's license. There is nothing to read, write, or play with. We interact with only the distraction of other families visiting at the tables around us. But they do not disturb us much.

As soon as we sat down yesterday, I saw the dull coldness in Simms's eyes. I felt the oppressive air around us trying to swallow us up.

"How are you emotionally?" I asked, hoping to soften the space between us.

"I have to be hard in here, Mom. There's no place for my emotions. What I'm learning in here—how I have to be to survive—is bad. I have to be somebody else, a person I never want to be when I get out of here. I hate what I have to do in here and how I have to be. I just hope I don't completely lose the person I want to be while I'm here. I hope I can find him again when I get out."

We talked about Simms's concern that immersion in the prison environment could potentially reprogram his tendencies.

"You will not allow this experience to destroy you or turn you into someone you don't want to be," I spoke firmly, looking deeply into his droopy eyes. It was cold in the room, and I started to shiver a little, but I tightened my muscles and continued.

"Be strong, Simms. You are not going to become a bad person. We are going to keep believing that you will be okay."

Simms sat staring at me, motionless. I could see he was weary by the way he slumped down in the chair. Usually, he sat straight, but on that day, he drooped.

"Right?"

"Right," he said with a complacent nod.

We hugged for a long time that day, and I said a silent prayer that Simms would find some relief. "I love you, Simms."

"Love you too, Mom.

A few weeks before the end of Rhett's college semester, things came to a head in New York. From Rhett's perspective, the lacrosse program was not living up to its end of the bargain, and bad management had caused him unnecessary injuries because he had not received adequate uniform padding before the first game. The coach's story was that Rhett showed telltale signs of substance abuse, including missing practices, not going to class or turning in assignments, arguing with teammates, and often sleeping all day in his dorm. Ultimately, Rhett decided the New York plan was not right for him, and he returned home.

As time passed, I realized Rhett and I could not live harmoniously together. Rhett was not receptive to my way of handling our differences or to my suggestions about what he should do as a member of our household. Wanting to give him every chance for progress and success, I considered that he might take initiative again if given another opportunity for independence.

I asked Rhett if he wanted to rent the lower unit of the house as a private apartment. He said yes, and we negotiated a reasonable rate. I moved upstairs, hoping the change would motivate Rhett and encourage self-reliance. And for a while, I thought it did.

But then something went wrong.

Whenever I tried to talk to Rhett and prod him in a healthy direction, he pushed me away with insults and accusations. Nevertheless, I hoped and waited for improvement.

April 22, 2019

Dear Mom,

I just got moved into a new cell—finally! It gets great radio reception, so I can listen to NPR again. This cell block is pretty good. I have made a couple of friends and get along with almost everyone. Not too much violence in here so far. I was excited to finally get a job, but doing laundry in the prison warehouse is disgusting—a total drag. But I am sticking to it— the price of staying in a nice block, plus being able to go home sooner. Even though I could potentially get out next August— just a little more than a year from now—it seems like a lifetime away.

Still no word back about the correspondence course. I might have missed the deadline for this year, but I'll try again next year, I guess. I haven't been able to work out much over the last few weeks. We haven't been going outside, and the gym equipment was locked up. They wouldn't let me keep the hardcover art book you sent me because it was too big. All books have to be smaller than a piece of standard paper. I'm going to look for *Hatchet* and *My Side of the Mountain* for a re-read since they were such good stories.

I've been talking to Rhett a lot on the phone. He seems

happy, and his girlfriend is going to work on finding me a pen pal. I hope it works out.

Did I tell you how I'm pretty sure I have permanent nerve damage in my arm? It's from my cellmate in jail constantly hitting my elbow, trying to get my funny bone. Now, it drives me crazy from my elbow to my pinky finger. It constantly falls asleep in a way that's definitely not normal. Just one more thing driving me batshit crazy in here! I'm afraid I might have to fight this for the rest of my life. Just thinking about it makes me want to cry. It hurts when I'm reading, and I can feel a lump of swollen nerves in my left elbow when comparing it to my right one. The lump is sensitive to touch and hurts when I press it.

Stuff like this (and being in prison) makes me want to hurt myself more because I am so angry at myself for making life so hard—and so goddamn miserable. It makes me hate myself. I know I don't and shouldn't, but I can't help it. I know it's stuff I can't control. So, I should let it go, but I just can't. Sometimes, I feel so helpless it stresses me out more than I can put into words. It is the worst thing I can feel—worse than any physical pain. I want to hurt so this feeling will go away, to stop the goddamn voices. I mean, I know it's in my head, and I am not really hearing voices, but it feels like I am. I know what people mean when they say they hear voices.

I don't want to give you a bad impression. I'm fine—as good as I can be in here. I won't do anything stupid, and I feel the same as I have every day since I've been locked up. It's nothing new, but it makes me feel crazy, even though I know I'm not. There are tons of people in here who really are crazy, and the psychiatric treatment here is a joke. This place doesn't even offer substance abuse classes or programs—at all! It all just stresses me to a point that seems unsustainable, especially if I had to be in here any longer than I do. I think the stress would literally kill me—the way Dad died. And the nerve damage in my arm thing, just like my being in prison, is for such a stupid reason—so avoidable and preventable, with painful, long-term consequences.

And the fact that no one is trying to make the system better, even though it's so widely understood to be broken, further compounds my frustration. People snap in here all the time. Just yesterday, someone lost it and attacked a guy with a knife— fighting over a cigarette. Two weeks ago, a guy attacked the police because he thought they were plotting to "get him." He was going around asking people what the cops had been saying about him, trying to figure out why they wanted to get him. We all tried to tell him that he was wrong about it—to no avail.

I know I need to meditate and draw, and do stuff to cope. I do. It's the only reason I have made it this far. But sometimes, stress and insanity insist on taking their turns, and I give in to the lunacy of the moments snailing by, leaving their slimy tracks like bad blood on the walls. I do the best I can—just trying to express what being here does to a person, to me. I'm sure my nerve damage wouldn't bother me if I was free.

Love you, Mom. And despite everything, I'm still doing okay.

Love,
Simms

May 7, 2019
Dear Simms,

I got your letter and found the words heavy, as you warned me they would be. For this reason, I read quickly and dropped the messages through a one-way valve into my heart, hoping to trap the details of your suffering until I could manage the weight of your pain. I have to be happy and hopeful—for all of us. That was the message on repeat in my mind until sleep took me somewhere else.

You called yesterday, excited to tell me that you finally got a job working in the warehouse doing laundry.

"It feels so good to be exhausted from actually doing something," you told me.

You also got transferred from the leaky cell, where the toilet was clogged and your bed was always wet and sour. They moved you to a working cell, where you are hoping the interactions will be better. Previously, you were in a nonworking-gang cell. A perk from the move is that you got moved to the side, where the reception for the radio is better. It was a great day. On top of all the other good news, you got to go outside and work out! I think you even got to use weights, but I'm not sure about that part. I'm so thankful that you can get out of your cell more often and be around other people with jobs.

"And there was a cool guy working the library too," your voice trailed on with more good news, and I could see you standing tall with your head high as you allowed a bit of hope to trickle into your broken spirit. "I think I'll be able to go by there most days on my way from work to my cell," you chimed with a smile in your voice that I could see through the telephone.

And relief that poured from your lips wrapped around my heart like a warm fuzzy blanket as I relished in the shared celebration of small victories.

Love,
Mom

~

May 10, 2019
Dear Mom,

I wanted to write and wish you a happy Mother's Day! When I come home, I'll take you out for a nice dinner to make up for missing three of them. I guess it will have to be something really fancy! With this letter, I have included a couple of drawings of people, as you recommended to me. I'm pretty proud of them. I really enjoyed the Whitey Bulger book you sent, and I am looking forward to the Grateful Dead book, too. Mostly, I'm excited to see you Friday. My new release date should be online now.

And WOW! The warehouse is hard work! Not sure if it's making time go faster or slower yet, but it's definitely taking a lot out of me. I am sure, in time, the perks will make up for the work I put in. But for now, I am just trying to keep at it so I can make it home sooner.

I have received a few letters from the guy who initiated the robbery against me. He has been begging for me to testify for him. And I guess he wants me to say he didn't do it. His family offered me money and stuff too. As much as I have forgiven him for it, I still cannot forget what he did that led to my deep depression and led to me doing things to end up back here. I can't help but feel like I may have been spared this hell if he had not done that to me, which leads me to feeling resentment that I have not been able to let go of yet. Plus, I definitely do not want to have to travel back to Wilmington to go to court, even if I wanted to help him.

Thanks again for everything, Mom. Happy Mother's Day! Love you more than anything in the world!

Love,
Simms

CHAPTER 19

June 9, 2019

Dear Simms,

You called to check on me, since I missed our visitation appointment. Of course, you were understanding and supportive of the change. It was one of those times when I wish I could have been in both places at once. After our phone conversation, I researched chess books for a bit. It was a lot of information, so I let it sit for a while. Eventually, I knew which ones I should order. One was on chess history, and two others covered games. I'm hoping you get some enjoyment out of them. So glad you have the art books! Now, if I can just find a sketchbook the authorities will allow.

Today, I'll be heading back to Morganton from my friend's place in the mountains because I have to turn the short-term rentals over. Rhett has training for a new job this week, so I might also need to help him with transportation. Then, I'll see you on Friday if all goes as planned.

I'm feeling very grateful for the hosting business, as it is allowing me time for writing. And speaking of writing, I'm determined to get back on a good schedule with my writing to you. Going with the flow and following my nature on the writing schedule is something I'm working on right now. What I am learning these days is that I must allow it to evolve naturally. I maintain my vision without forcing myself into a rigorous schedule. I simply try to write consistently and trust that something good will come of it.

Sometimes, I feel so incapable of writing creatively. I write anyway. Rather than letting it overwhelm me with doubt, I remind myself that I am capable of expressing my thoughts. I just need to stop having expectations about those thoughts. I must knead them with love and watch them take shape without comparing them to the thoughts of others.

I read others' writing and find myself amazed by their expressive abilities. Maybe it is time for me to take a break from reading so much. Allowing myself room to write without the words of others hanging so closely in my mind could give me space to trust myself, to hear and feel what I am supposed to be writing.

Presently, I'm at Grant's house. Remember the retired pilot I mentioned, who came through my Airbnb when he was in the area shopping for a house—the really tall artist guy? Well, he ended up moving from Florida a couple months ago.

Since then, we've been spending quite a bit of time together, going back and forth between my house and his. And it has been fun to have a playmate again.

The view from Grant's house is completely enveloped in a cloud as I write this. And the birds have quieted. So, I leave my computer to hike up the mountain.

The grade is steep, and my heart rate rises rapidly by the time I reach the end of the short driveway. I'll hike to the top and feel refreshed. The roadside is clothed in newly formed blackberries, more than I could pick. In another month, right around my birthday, they will burst with deep purple. I am thrilled at the thought of a bountiful harvest. Grant and I are the only ones on the mountain most of the time, but a few other families reside nearby part time. It's very likely that I am the only person interested in the blackberry harvest. Although the groundskeeper, Orilio, might be eyeing them too. Either way, there is plenty for us and the animals. There are thousands of berries, untouched by chemicals and pesticides. Wish you were here, so we could pick them together.

You'll be excited to know that there are apple and nut trees here too! Sometimes, when I am out here, I wonder if I have died and gone to heaven. It is so peaceful. I look forward to coming out here with you because I know it will be like heaven to you as well. The region northwest of Asheville has lots of cows too. Yesterday, we went on a cow-watching adventure and visited a cemetery where almost everyone buried there was a Worley. I got lots of name ideas for my stories. We found black cows, cows with white faces, and cows that looked sort of whitish gray. They were my favorites because their coats were glossy, which accentuated the definition of their muscular bodies.

At one of our stops, there was a mature, black cow leading about a dozen other cows. The youngest calf looked about a year old and followed closely by her side. We stopped because the two were very near the road. They were alarmed by our interest and ran to join the others back from the road, on the other side of a small stream. After they retreated, the calf proceeded to initiate play with two other adolescents who were a little bigger. One of them greeted the calf enthusiastically, and they both plodded around for a couple of minutes before settling back into grazing. The youngest calf continued to try his luck at play, to the obvious annoyance of some of the older cows, who overtly rejected his efforts by nudging him away or turning from him.

Watching the herd change formation was interesting. One cow thought she had a pretty sweet plot of grass. Each time another would come into her grazing space, she would nudge them away. The pregnant cow roamed off to find respite under a large shade tree, a little distance from the herd. But I saw her keeping an eye out.

A steady rain came and deterred my hike up the mountain, so I will try again later. I look forward to going on some cow-watching adventures with you after your release. Maybe we can find a good spot for you near Asheville. Who knows? Maybe I will work my way further west by then too. I love you, son!

Love,

Mom

June 10, 2019

Dear Mom,

It's just another day in here. I'm trying to stay positive and convince myself that thirteen more months is not a long time. But that's hard when every month feels like an eternity. I have decided that time went more quickly when I didn't have a super shitty job, as the weekends go by with relative quickness. I dread going to work every day. Mondays and Wednesdays are the absolute bane of my existence.

I'm trying to put in productive writing time with this letter today. Most books and movies about prison paint an intriguing picture about prison while never truly conveying the almost indescribable psychological impact incarceration has on inmates. In contrast to the exciting and interesting stories about prison, the truth is that it is painfully and depressingly monotonous. Every day is maddeningly similar. The only exciting events to break up the tedious monotony are random acts of violence—fights, gang beatings, stabbings, etc. You would think that something so boring would not be stressful, but the opposite is true. For one thing, most everyone in here is agitated due to crowded, unsanitary conditions. Violence and brutality are such a significant part of life that people's first reflex to any situation is violence as a defense mechanism.

It is stressful to worry about family matters and most other things that are everyday worries to free people. This is because I feel unable to influence or contribute to solutions. I worry about you and Rhett every day and think regretfully about the emotional and financial burden on you as a result of my incarceration. And even though I have a full-time job, I only make five dollars a week. I worry about Rhett getting into trouble and think about how I want to be a good role model for him. Then, I find myself spiraling down again into a pit of shame, reminded of how my incarceration is setting a horrible example. I stress about the possibility of being victimized by violence in here—like how I was extorted, then beaten severely by gang members on my first day in prison. As a result of that beating, I was demoted to close custody, thrown to the bottom of the proverbial prison bucket and left there to wallow in my own animal filth, wondering if I could ever pick my less-than-human shell up out of the mud. I'm terrified by the increased risk of violence now upon me in this hellhole—and by the consequences of an extended sentence as a result of the regular and unavoidable violence.

One almost unbelievable practice in North Carolina prisons is punishing people for needing protective custody. If you tell the police that you need to be moved because you feel unsafe or because you are being threatened, they will give you a write-up and place you in solitary confinement. Then, you are charged ten dollars for receiving a write-up. Additionally, you lose canteen and phone privileges, lose your job if you have one, and sometimes even get time added to your sentence. Yes, these are all repercussions for requesting protection from violent inmates when you are incarcerated in a North Carolina prison. As a result of these circumstances, I must learn to live in the violence and survive it—along with many others. Meanwhile, I hope and pray that I can hold on to some measure of sanity through the process. The anticipation of living on the outside terrifies me too. Will I be able to face regular people on the street?

A boulder of fear tumbles toward me, and I try to stand against it with my bow drawn. Paralyzed in my bunk, I will myself to a sitting position, will myself to move, to read, to write. I thwart the boulder today and pray that I can overcome the avalanche tomorrow. After that, I don't know. I can't think about it. Today, tomorrow, the dark tunnel between me and freedom—sweet, terrifying freedom. God, please let me find a way to lock the doors of bondage forever when I reach the light on the other side. Don't let it suck me in again. Please.

Although I practice many stress-control techniques, I still feel this ordeal is taking years off my life. And frustration over the legal system's current approach to substance abuse doesn't help matters. Being forced to experience drug withdrawal from being incarcerated does not treat addiction, even though it may get people "off" the drugs. The cold turkey method often leads to serious symptoms of PAWS, one of the most common precursors to relapse of drug abuse. In successful recovery programs, drug addicts make negative associations related to the addictive substances. This is one of the most important steps toward true recovery. When external circumstances such as incarceration force abrupt, involuntary withdrawal from addictive substances, the addict does not make these negative associations. As a result of this process, an addict's risk of relapse is significant, and rehabilitation potential is stalled.

Under these circumstances, addicts blame law enforcement, incarceration, and other people for their circumstances—not the drugs. The addict is less able to make a direct association between his drug abuse and undesirable outcomes. Instead, uncontrollable cravings take center stage in the addicted mind, distorting reality in favor of the object of his desire—the addictive substance that relieves his craving. This distorted thinking is exacerbated by the lack of effective rehabilitation programs available to inmates.

Effective recovery programs help addicts end their relationship with the addictive substance by encouraging and guiding the process of closure. When an addict doesn't participate intrinsically in the process of withdrawal, there is no closure to the relationship. Therefore, the addict feels an overwhelming desire to reunite with the substance in order to experience equilibrium, comfort, familiarity, belonging.

Closure is just as important when ending an unhealthy relationship with drugs as it is when ending an unhealthy relationship with another person. In unhealthy human relationships, an abrupt, involuntary end to the connection may result in feelings of disequilibrium. Routines are upset, and a person's sense of stability is shaken. One or both people feel a need for the familiar, despite any unpleasant side effects of such familiarity. Humans need to feel some measure of control over their own circumstances. Without personal reflection and internal development toward positive changes, an addict cannot move forward with confidence into the domain of true recovery.

Instead, he finds himself on a runaway train to nowhere, unable to do anything but watch his impending doom as the momentum builds toward a massive derailment. And each time the train runs away, the addict can only hope that the result will not be his ultimate demise. Closure in recovery is a complex, personal, and often painful process. But it is critical. And so many factors affect closure for recovering addicts. Hopefully, the sharing of my personal experiences related to this topic will provide some understanding and encouragement to families challenged with similar circumstances.

All my love,
Simms

~

June 19, 2019

Dear Simms,

Your last letter was amazing! Thank you for putting such effort into personal expression. I understood very well your concern about possibly having to deal with a physical condition for the rest of your life because I have had that same concern in my life too. When my neck pain was at its worst, I remember finding a book written by a woman who described her malady as very similar to mine. I bought the book and devoured, expecting to find answers. It never occurred to me she might write an entire book about chronic pain without having found some solution, something that would ease it.

It devastated me when I finished the book only to realize the author never found relief. Sobbing in despair, I could feel the last bit of hope seeping out of me. *What's the point of living with all this pain?* I had asked myself. *How can I keep smiling and being pleasant day after day while the pain gnaws at me like a rat chewing on a floorboard?* But I knew I must pick myself up, put the pain out of my mind, and keep going. I had to keep smiling and trying to find a solution.

Something deep within compelled me to persevere, even though every day began with pain, and every day ended with pain. The space between was just a blur of putting one foot in front of the other, faking it the best I could to avoid pulling others into the darkness of my affliction.

A few days later, I found some fight in me and signed up for hot yoga, knowing I had tried all the conventional medical options aside from surgery. I didn't want to go that route yet because I had seen others end up worse off from surgical intervention. Before I read that book, I had tried cortisone shots in my shoulders and neck. It was a painful process that involved a very long needle, and I took it with a smile, hoping it would relieve my pain. When it didn't help, I realized I would have to help my body heal itself through holistic practices.

I experienced life-changing results after practicing yoga five days a week for a month and implementing strict dietary practices. At the end of January 2015, I awoke one morning pain free! It was like being born again. Everything in the world looked new and bright.

I believe your body can recover from the trauma of incarceration. Meanwhile, eat your vegetables and take care of your body as well as you can.

Devotedly, with much love,
Mom

~

June 20, 2019

Dear Simms,

Today, I want to write you a happy letter. I missed your calls yesterday. Hopefully, you will get to try again today. I know Wednesdays are a really hard day at work for you. For this reason, I'm glad it's Thursday. You made it through another hump day.

Right now, I'm in the mountains at Grant's place. Yesterday, after hiking to the top of Whisper Mountain to see if any blackberries were ripe yet, Grant and I hiked down a trail that passes by his house near a creek. On the way back up, we encountered a copperhead. It's the first one I've seen since moving to North Carolina, even in all my hiking adventures. He saw it coiled up beside the trail next to a tree trunk.

He said, "Snake," and pointed the tip of his umbrella in that direction.

So, by the time I saw the snake, it was hissing and coiled to strike in response to the pointing umbrella.

"Run!" I yelled as my legs started spinning. With eyes still on the snake instead of where my feet were going, I tripped over myself and went down like a classic cartoon.

Isn't it interesting how fear manages to hurt us before the perceived threat? Nevertheless, we both escaped without a snake bite and had a good laugh.

Love,

Mom

CHAPTER 20

As I stumbled along through the grieving process and navigated turbulent terrain with my sons, I developed the coping strategy of writing letters to Ben. Parenting our boys alone was a daunting task that intensified my grief in times when I believed I had failed. Before his death, I had been counting on Ben's experience and wisdom to lead us through that part of our family's journey. So, when things did not work out that way, I resorted to writing through my emotional pain—a habit I developed as a freshman in high school when my English teacher required me to write a personal journal entry every day.

Each time the pain of missing Ben became unbearable, I was compelled toward a space between my world and his, a place where I could talk to him—and he would hear me. I knew a way to that place because I had visited it many times while he was alive, whenever he would retreat into the private lair of his soul —in silence. In those days, I would write to him about our troubles and what I thought we should do as I waited for him to emerge.

Without knowing what I was doing at the time, in writing letters to Ben throughout our relationship, I had created a world where Ben would always be just around the corner, watching a ball game. So, after he passed away, writing letters to him was not only as natural as breathing; it was a clear path to the space between our worlds—a place where he would never die.

∾

June 21, 2019

Dear Ben,

You visited me in my dreams last night, and it was so very nice to have your arms around me. What strikes me about dreams of you is how we communicate without speech, as we often did when you were alive. In this dream, you missed me, and I missed you. It's like we knew we couldn't be together for some reason, but I wasn't exactly sure why. I probably thought it was because you needed space to be yourself, without the responsibilities of having a wife. I'm glad you do not have to feel that weight anymore, even though you carried it with great dignity and grace. Your love was so pure and true.

Love,

Champ

∾

June 25, 2019

Dear Ben,

Yesterday, I was home alone for the first time in a while. I mentioned in my last letter that you came to visit me recently in my dreams. I love it when you do that. You're always such a gentleman about the fact that we aren't married anymore because of your passing away. I wonder how I would feel in your situation, watching you with someone else. I would want you to be happy and loved—to have all that you ever wanted, all that you gave up for the sake of our marriage.

It has been a long road trying to figure out how to be good

for myself—and good for those I love. I am grateful for your patient love and how it sustained me through so many treacherous years of trying to love myself. Why was it so hard to love myself? You were such a strong and constant warmth, my life-sized teddy bear. I miss your arms more than words can say. As much as you seemed complacent and distracted, you welcomed me when I wiggled into that sweet place over your heart and wrapped my arms around you. It was my favorite place in the world for twenty-seven years. Even during the hardest times of our marriage, it was always where I wanted to be.

So, if I were in your place now, I would be the same as you have been to me—supportive—despite the fact that I miss you and remember fondly how close we were in the end. I finally understood your humor and played with your sarcasm rather than taking your comments as insults. I could see that it made you feel loved and accepted when your natural behavior did not make me feel inadequate. I had learned so well how to read your moods, how to be a good wife to you. And it brought me such joy and satisfaction to know I was finally making up for all the trouble I put you through as I was growing up.

Even though our relationship was at its best for several years before you passed away, my heart was breaking for you. I could see the pain in your eyes and feel it in your heart. You worried about the boys and realized that you could not protect them from youthful foolishness as much as you wished you could. When Simms went to jail, you were devastated. You were never a drunk, but alcohol was your medication of choice, and I could feel it wearing away at your body.

Sometimes, I wonder if my perception of this made it worse or caused it to be so—especially because I encouraged you to get a comprehensive cognitive evaluation. I could see changes in you that told me something was wrong. And, in hindsight, I understand. Your cognition was affected, as I suspected, because the blocked arteries of your heart severely restricted blood flow to your brain and body. Just because I saw changes in you and encouraged you to go to the doctor and get evaluated does not mean I made you sick. I just wish a doctor would have detected your heart condition before the fatal event.

I guess that's all for now, though I don't remember if there was something specific I was planning to write about. Yesterday, I passed by Tweetsie Railroad on my way to Boone and reminisced about the times we went there with the boys. They loved riding the train through the mountains and watching the cowboys put on a show with cap guns and western hats.

I love you, Honey!

Champp

~

July 23, 2019

Dear Ben,

It's Tuesday at the Grind Cafe, so they're playing classic country, and I am making the best of it. Although, bless your heart, you could not two-step to save your life. I have to give you credit for trying, though. It was a hoot when we took those lessons together. From then on, I was happy if you danced with me at all, even if we just held each other and swayed from side to side in one place. I miss you, and the sting of it rises in my throat until my nose burns. You visited me last night in my dreams. But it was one of those times when I felt inadequate.

In reality, I did my best, and you did too. We loved each other the way we knew how, and that makes our love valid. We stuck it out and did what we thought was right and good. It drove me bananas the way you were so closed, but you were a man of outstanding character. Your love and devotion provided a remarkable life for me and the boys. Thank you, Ben.

Yours truly,

Champ

June 21, 2019

Simms called and told me all his care package items had been stolen by a gang after the police searched his things and left them scattered all over the floor. He was devastated about losing his peanut butter and coffee, both small comforts in the midst of a hostile existence. He had just received the care package a few days before.

The police search resulted in charges against Simms for having too much ibuprofen. He also got a charge for damage to a jacket and for having a lock that was not on his locker, if I remember correctly.

"It's impossible to be good in here," he said. "Doing right things only gets you further extorted by the gangs. Reporting extortion gets you put in solitary confinement where you're completely isolated and treated like the scum of the earth. There's no winning in here. It's just a matter of trying to play a crazy game with no rules the best you can. And even then, you lose every freakin' day."

He lost phone privileges and was sentenced to solitary anyway. However, there is a wait for solitary, so he's hoping he'll finish the program and get shipped out before a space opens up. Prisoners find ways to share calls, so I've still been able to speak to him, and that's a relief. When I can't hear his voice or visit him, it's excruciating because I don't know if he's okay. It's not like the prison calls to let you know what's going on. So, when he isn't able to call or have visitors, it's nerve-racking—wondering if he got attacked, wondering if he has been critically injured. And there's no way to find out these things—at least none that I know about. I guess they'd call if he died. But short of that, there's nothing to do but wait until I hear from him.

Right now, he's at rock bottom. Holding out not to join a gang is continual punishment. One person can't stand against them, so he is left with only one option—to allow them to extort him completely, making his life miserable. It's bad enough being in prison without much comfort of any sort. Then, add the continual abuse he gets from gangs—waking him up in the night, taking whatever they want, showing whatever aggression they want while the police turn away.

Maybe minimum-security prisons have it better, but that's no consolation for inmates who are in medium or close custody. Simms is not a violent criminal. Do I think he is completely innocent? Of course not! I am aware of what he has done. I believe he has been honest with me about that. Furthermore, I raised him and know him pretty well. He is a kind, intelligent human being who has a propensity for deviance. But isn't there some way to help him? He has a beautiful heart and soul. He wants to stay out of trouble. Doesn't that count for something? It's frustrating to me—and to him. We both want to solve this problem because we both want him to live a good life—a free life without trouble.

God, please help Simms find a way to stay out of trouble when he is released.

Early July 2019

Simms called and told me that they wrote him up for having too many family photos. As a result, he might not be allowed to receive calls for a month. Somehow, he got in to see the person who works on transferring inmates. He expressed his concern about the recent write-up and how it might affect his new status as medium custody. She told him not to worry about it, so he expects to be relocated soon. I'm eager to hear from him and find out where he will be. It's been a blessing to have him only an hour away in Taylorsville because we have been able to have regular contact visits every other week.

I'm hopeful that the transfer will go through without any drama because it seems like he really needs something to go his way. He was at a very low point after our visit when he returned to his cell to find it in shambles. The write-up for too many photos was a blow. He sometimes gets completely overcome with the fear that, despite his very best efforts, the law will always find a way to bring him down. I hope and pray that he can learn how to live a peaceful life without getting into trouble with the law. It hurts me to see his struggle. I have to believe that he can and will find peace and freedom. I want him to believe it too.

Please, God. Help us.

CHAPTER 21

July 10, 2019

Dear Simms,

Today, I fought the urge to withdraw. You called, and I felt afraid to answer. I had an uneasy feeling about what's going on with you. Your stolen phone card whispers, "There is something else to the story," and I do not want to know what.

Ultimately, I must be able to say no to some things without feeling guilty. When I finally swiped the green dot to answer, an electronic voice said your call money was out. I will not add more right now. Instead, I'll visit you on Friday.

There is so much I can't say. Retreating to the wilderness is more tempting each day. I want to stay strong, but I'm weary. I feel anxious when things change for you and we cannot talk openly on the phone (or in letters). I know you must play by different rules to survive in there, and I must protect myself. When my gut warns me that something is wrong, I have to trust myself and wait until more information is available.

I tell myself, *I am not afraid*. I imagine your father being here to relieve some of the pressure. However, I realize it would not ease my burden because he would be hurting about it too. We would both be hurting for you—and for ourselves. I have to keep believing you will be able to live a peaceful, free life after you serve your time.

Ultimately, we all must bear our own burdens. No matter how close we are to others, each of us endures what we must. And no amount of closeness to another person can carry the load for us. Every human who wakes up and tries to live another day has courage. You are brave and strong, my son. Thank you for loving and accepting me, even when I say no to some of your requests. I look forward to seeing you Friday and clarifying what is going on with your stolen phone card.

Love,

Mom

~

July 13, 2019

When I awoke this morning, I started reflecting on conversations with Simms—which led me to wondering how he can get into so much trouble despite being such a nice person. Amid my pondering, a relevant story from my childhood came to mind.

The desks were arranged like a table, with about eight students seated in a rectangular array. I can't remember what type of activity we were doing, but Mr. Everett was conducting the lesson. I was in a playful mood and slightly bored with the objective, as I recall. Another student had a little change purse on her desk. We were all giggling and playing because the activity had not started yet. Without thinking about it, I took the little change purse and hid it under my leg, in my chair. I intended this as a game and expected the person to notice that it was missing. I anticipated her looking for it, and I would present it to her quickly, to her relief. What I had not anticipated was that she would immediately get upset and tell the teacher that someone had stolen her purse.

Money was not something I had much dealings with at that time in my life. It had no value to me, as I recall. I did not bring money for lunch. Nor did I have any money to spend, think about, or dream about. Instead, I dreamed about ripe blackberries on the high line, and red plums on the trees that lined the cow pasture.

Before I knew what was happening, there was a seriousness in the air. Someone had stolen the girl's money. Meanwhile, here I was with the little purse underneath me, wondering how to get out of this sticky situation. A moment ago, I was a good friend playing with my classmates. Now, I was a criminal, a thief, a bad and horrible person. Furthermore, every moment that the purse was missing, Mr. Everett and the other students seemed to become more serious. Someone had committed a terrible crime, and a confession must be made. The little pouch bulged under my leg, hot and mean, as I tried to figure my way out. Blood rushed into my ears, striking like someone trying to pound a tunnel through a rocky mountain. In an instant, everything had gone wrong.

Eventually, Mr. Everett went around to each of us with a search. He asked me to stand up, and there was the little pouch, pointing its mean little corners at me, accusing me. I felt the silent stares of those who were my friends just moments ago. Just like that, I was a bad girl, a thief, someone who could not be trusted. Hot, salty tears threatened to burst from my eyes as the lecture ensued. I had no words of defense. In fact, I had no words at all. The complexity of it all swirled in my head as I tried to figure how everything had gone so wrong. I was ashamed, embarrassed, and bewildered.

The hardest thing was that nobody asked for an explanation, or even thought one was needed. Everyone seemed to know what I had not known—that I stole money because I wanted something that wasn't mine. It wasn't true. I knew that. But all I could think about is that everyone else seemed to know much more about the matter than I did. Confused and humiliated, I plodded through the day as an outcast, wondering how to get my life back on track. But lacking the words I needed to explain my case, all I could do was cry.

~

July 25, 2019

Dear Simms,

I called this morning to schedule a visit and found out that you were moved to Mountain View Correctional in Spruce Pine, North Carolina. I felt emotional as I considered the transfer itself and your apprehension about changing social dynamics. My heart aches for you, and I hope that you will find a bit of relief from the circumstances that have been tearing away at your positive disposition. I have watched you struggle to hold on to your sanity by frail strands, smiling as much as you could, for both our sakes. I have looked deeply into your strained eyes and felt your aching heart.

I have asked myself, *Will he break into irreparable pieces before he gets out of there?*

I went through my day handling business for the short-term rentals, some electrical repairs, and cleaning. All the while, I thought of you, acclimating to your new environment. It must be overwhelming, even if it's better, in some ways. After all, you will be in the regular population again, a situation that was certainly cause for anxiety at Polk. Despite the fact that it's a medium security facility, your roommates are criminal males, cooped up in a small space together, irritated, frustrated, afraid, angry. Nevertheless, I pray that something will be better for you there.

You called this afternoon, but the conversation was cut short. You told me you had gotten some outside time, the place is extremely crowded, someone robbed you, and some of your writing was confiscated because it was about drugs. Of course, you were upset. I pray that as you settle in, you will find yourself in a situation that is more bearable than before—that you find a way to have some joy in whatever small things this relocation offers. I am thankful that you are still only an hour away from me, so at least we can continue to visit in person on a regular basis.

You were finally able to call again yesterday evening. You told me there are over one hundred men in your block. You have a cell with one roommate. Unfortunately, he's a crack addict and brings others into your cell to smoke. Since you are new, the police barged in and searched you. You told them it wasn't you, but they took a lot of your writing that you were working on for our book because it was about drugs. I could hear the anxiety in your voice, but you held it together, trying not to alarm me too much.

I'm at the Grind Cafe, drinking coffee. It's a beautiful morning, so I rode up here on my bicycle to get my writing done before I go home to clean upstairs. A few familiar faces come by and greet me, which feels nice. Living in this town brings me joy because the people are friendly, and I feel a sense of belonging like I've never felt in any other town.

Yesterday, I harvested almost a quart of blueberries and a few tomatoes. I planted peppers and tomatoes this year because I knew they would have a good chance of success without my coddling. They would have appreciated a bit of water now and then, but I refused. Despite my negligence, they have produced a steady harvest, for which I am grateful.

I'm hoping and praying that things improve for you at Mountain View and that you get transferred, if that's the best thing. You told me that your radio doesn't work at all there, which is no surprise because of the location. My cell service is one of the best, but I can't get a signal around those parts, either. It made me laugh when you said you may as well have brought a brick, referring to your radio. You have your father's sense of humor, which makes my whole being smile. Through the hardest time of your life, you can still make a joke—and that's impressive.

I'm so proud of you, son. Hang in there. You are making good progress. Something will give. We have to keep believing that. Right now, I'm going to imagine you with a much better roommate situation and opportunities to rest in peace, write, study, and soak up some fresh mountain air.

Much love,
Mom

~

August 3, 2019

I drove away from my visit to Mountain View Correctional Institute in Spruce Pine, North Carolina, hoping Simms would call soon. When we sat down to visit, I noticed his body was tense and asked what was wrong.

"The guards just told me they're about to search my room," Simms said with a strained voice and wide eyes. He leaned back in his chair for a deep breath and added, "They were putting on gloves and saying it was going to be a lot to sort through. I'm so freaked out. I don't think I can take it if they send me back to close custody." Simms closed his eyes and took another deep breath, rubbed his hand over his heart, and exhaled before continuing. "I feel helpless, like nothing is within my control."

I watched his jaws tighten, his brows furrow, and his eye dart while we tried to converse. Meanwhile, my heart raced with anxiety. *Will they send him back to Alexander? Will they add more time to his sentence? Why is this happening? What did he do? Is he telling me everything?*

"I feel like it's impossible to stay out of trouble in here, even when I try to do everything right. They just keep poking me like a caged animal, amusing themselves at my expense. Why won't they just leave me alone and let me finish my time?" Simms said in a broken voice that cut at my heart like a shard of glass.

"I understand your fear because it hovers over me as well," I said, trying to soothe him with a soft voice. "I know you'll get through this and find some peace. Something good will happen," I said, trying to assure us both.

"I can hardly endure it each day, Mom. Every single day feels unbearable." Simms clenched his jaw and rubbed both his hands over his face. "Violence is everywhere, and drug abuse is pervasive. It feels like roaches crawling around, and I can't get away from them. They invade at every opportunity. They come into my cell looking around, trying to take what they can. It's a hellhole."

His words tore at my heart and muted me.

Simms called that night and told me they wrote him up for having too many family photos. When I asked if there was more to the story, he said he couldn't talk about it on the phone. The transition from Alexander to Mountain View was taking its toll on Simms, but at least he didn't get sent back to close custody.

CHAPTER 22

September 12, 2019

Dear Simms,

I went to see you for two weeks in a row, and yesterday, you called to ask if I would come again this weekend. Our last visit was not very long because the guards could not locate you. I waited for almost an hour before you came to the visitation room. There is a definite problem with procedures in calling for prisoners, but I am glad I got to see you for a little while. I had told you on the phone to be careful and watch your back because of some suspicious visitors who tried to talk to me about you. I wasn't sure what was going on. However, after I told you to be careful, I thought you might worry too much, so I decided to come see you off our regular schedule in order to explain the whole thing to you about the woman and her supposed husband whom she visits there.

The woman says that her son is in prison too, but not at Mountain View, where you are currently. He is somewhere near the coast. She asked me if you had ever done drugs, and if I ever send you money. She asked if you are a member of a gang and said that her son joined a gang in prison. She said that her husband told her about you and how you were put in the gang and drug unit. At first, when I told you about her, you said she was mistaken, and that you are in a different unit than the one she thought. She gave me the name of someone to call and said that I should try to get you moved because of extortion. You said you wanted to stay in that unit. Eventually, because of something her husband said or did, the police came to you and asked if you wanted to be relocated to another cell block. You opted to stay where you are because you have settled there and don't want to risk being put somewhere worse. You have connected with a couple of guys intellectually in your current cell block. Moving would be risky because you might not connect with anyone in the new location and you would end up stuck without any fulfilling socialization. That could be devastating, since socialization is one of the few things you get in there.

You tried to explain to me why you wanted to stay where you are, and I told you that I trust you to do what is best for your survival and overall well-being. I respect you as an adult, and it is your business if you want to stay where you are. You are the one having to do the time, and you are an adult. I do not question your reasons or decisions. I just want to be supportive and encourage you to make the best of your time by continuing to write and do other healthy, productive things. I opened your most recent letter today and worked on transcribing some of your previous writing.

Recently, I told you that I would pay you five dollars per page for your writing. This is because I believe your ideas and writing are valuable. Additionally, I want to alleviate your feelings of frustration about not being able to work or carry your weight financially. I want you to understand that I take our collaboration on this book project seriously and consider it work. You have a legitimate job as a writer. We have to make this drama count for something by seeing our project through to the end. There is no other option. It is hard for me to read about your suffering, so I carry your letters around for a while, running from them a little, until I can breathe, read, and let myself feel.

Your letters and other writings about whatever is in your mind and heart are treasures to me. I cannot just scan the words with my eyes, or even my mind. I must take them like morsels of communion, poured from your soul as an offering. And so, I wait until I am able to give all of my attention to what you have written. I take the words, like babes, into my bosom. I wrap them in a soft blanket of gratitude and lay them on an altar of hope. I bathe them in warm tears, and anoint them with the salve of my prayers. As I type the letters you send, I feel the anguish of their birth, and my fingers dance upon the keyboard with gentle touches of validation.

I have read the first page of what you sent recently. And now, I will listen to the sound of your hand as it trembles upon the page. I see you lying on the cold concrete of your bare cell, pen in hand, aching elbow. You close out the distractions of boredom and the smells of men who have no hope. You see a tiny ray of light and harness its power in the blue ocean of your eyes, remembering the owl that came to you the other day. He was not there by chance, you know. He came to tell you something. What was it?

Your hand begins to move across the page, and you watch formless black ink tattoo itself along the whiteness. A trail of letters pushes your cramping hand along the smooth surface. Courageously, you carve a path along the dark ridges of your soul, tracing the shape of your heart, leaning on the light of the Life Giver. He takes your anger and frustration as the emotion of your condition squeezes your gut and tells you nothing is there— in the cold, spiritless air of your cell. The liar tells you that God has slighted you, but we know better.

You feel the warmth in your belly. You hear me answer the phone. We embrace and talk of cats, family, weather, philosophy, books, and the beauty of apples and mountains. We feel the pull of that Great Spirit of Life, compelling us to find our limits, to grow until we reach the edge of all we can be. That cannot be nothing. The liar is wrong, and His presence confirms that the surrounding air is not empty. God is there, and He is giving you strength to write one more page today, and another, and another. He is the Great Comforter, the Spirit of Boldness and Wisdom. He guides your hand and shines light upon the truth that you seek.

Write on, my son. Write on!

Love,

Mom

A Life-Changing Moment

By Simms

One moment that changed my life forever was when my father told me he had once been addicted to heroin. Although details before and after are blurry, that moment remains clear. I was eighteen and had mostly moved out of our house to live with my girlfriend, Kelly. However, I still maintained a room at my family's house. I showed up at the house for a few reasons— most specifically, heroin I had stashed in the house. For reasons that now escape me, my dad was arguing with me about drugs— drugs I, as an ignorant teenager, was convinced my dad did not know about, and did not know I was doing.

He had no proof of my drug use, but as my father and someone with knowledge about drug use, he knew I was using. He was heatedly counseling me about drug use and the company I was keeping. I was brushing him off as I collected my parcel of heroin. But when I came out of my room, he confronted me on the landing at the top of the stairs.

All I remember saying to him was, "Why do you care so

much?" which, looking back on it from where I am now, was possibly the most horrible thing I could say.

There were a million answers to this. He cared because he was my dad, because he loved me, because he wanted to see me do well, because he didn't want me to go and fuck up my life like I have now. He did not want me to waste my life rotting in prison like I am now. He did not want me to wake up every day wishing I had died already, wishing this endless misery would just be over, wishing I had never been born because the misery I feel is more intense than anything good I ever felt. There were so many options to make me happy, and I had to pick one that could make me feel this bad.

Of all the answers he could have given me, he found the one that would have the most profound impact on me. He said, "Because I was addicted to heroin."

I immediately felt a flood of emotions, followed by so many questions. My dad had offhandedly referred to his history of drug use and activity before. But for the most part, that area of his life was shrouded in mystery. The only dad I had ever known was a conservative, hard-working, honest man. From all I knew, he was the epitome of self-control.

Unfortunately, our conversation was cut short. Who knows what would have happened if we had continued that conversation? I can only hope that some other family might consider this and have the courage to continue the conversation. I went to jail, and my father passed away during my incarceration, but that was not the end of things for my family. This is why I am writing now. I am writing to make all the terrible things that have happened to me and my family count for something.

September 20, 2019

I had that motherly feeling of knowing that cannot be ignored. Although I was tired and looking forward to a few days of writing without any other obligations, I could not ignore the gnawing in my gut telling me to go see Simms. He had called a few days before to tell me he had been transferred to Pender Correctional Center for a three-month drug education program. When I asked about why he got transferred so suddenly, Simms said he had applied for various opportunities to earn time toward early release. But despite his explanation, I was concerned about the sudden changes and needed to see him.

I scheduled a visit and drove five hours to Burgaw to find out what was going on.

"Tell me about your relocation," I said, after burying my face in his curls for a long hug.

When he sat down across from me, his hands moved over his chest. I watched his torso expand with a breath and stop short with a wince. His hand stopped over his heart, and he curled up in a slump before trying again to sit upright.

"What's wrong?" I leaned in, considering him with scrutiny.

"I don't know. I just started feeling bad. My chest is tight, and I'm nauseous. I can't get a good breath."

He pushed the words out between grimaces and closed his eyes as he spoke. And despite his discomfort, he answered my questions about his condition. We were both worried but helpless to do anything except hope for the best. The guards read their computer screens without attention to the matter. Meanwhile, I thought he might fall over with a heart attack at any moment. Simms has always shown a high tolerance for pain, so seeing him in distress caused me great concern.

Because of the distance I had to travel, we qualified for an extended visit, which meant visiting for the usual two-hour block, leaving for a short break, and returning for another two-hour visit. As Simms told me about his transfer, he alternated positions between slumping and arching, stretching tall and putting his head on the table.

"I'm just trying to get comfortable," he said when I reached out to touch his arm. "I'll be okay in a few minutes. Maybe it's just indigestion."

I stared through anxious eyes and tried to hear what he said about the condition of Pender Correctional, but concern gripped me and squeezed my own heart until I felt like it might stop.

"Do you want me to come back for the second session?" I asked, unsure if he could sit up much more.

"Yes, please. I'll try to rest on the break and drink some water or something." With intensity, his deep blue eyes stared into mine. "Thanks for coming, Mom. It means the world to me just to see you and hug you. I feel better just because you're here."

When I returned from the fifteen-minute break, Simms's condition had not improved. We tried to pick up where we left off, but he could no longer talk. Fear shone on his face, which made me afraid too. And the chairs were hard and cold.

"I guess you need to go lie down," I said, not knowing what else to say or do.

We hugged goodbye, and I trudged toward the exit with an earnest prayer seeping from my heart, hoping a rest would rejuvenate him. Later, he told me they made him stay at the table until visitation ended almost two hours later. Meanwhile, the long road home across North Carolina rose and fell with apprehension and emotion.

CHAPTER 23

September 27, 2019

Dear Simms,

Ever since our last visit, I have been missing your calls and eager to hear from you. When I spoke with you today, you told me that they made you stay for the duration of visitation, anyway. So, at least we know we should have stuck it out. Seeing you sick distressed me, especially when the guards ignored the situation and made you stay at the table after I left. So, I guess it's official. When you go to prison, you are no longer treated like a human being. I witnessed it with my own eyes. On the other hand, I realize some inmates would exploit a system that showed sensitivity to their ailments.

It is also possible that they see sick inmates very often, especially in the drug program, where many prisoners might arrive and go through withdrawals. I just know you are not a hypochondriac, and you are very tolerant of sickness and pain. Therefore, when your suffering shows, I take it seriously. There must be some way to get better medical care. It seems like they could provide services upon request if a family member paid. But I guess that might stir up contention within the inmate population. Ultimately, it boils down to the fact that there are lifelong repercussions resulting from incarceration, including those related to profoundly limited medical and dental care.

This is especially unfortunate for people who are wrongfully convicted. I guess these are all judgment calls that someone must make, and I can see that it is a difficult dilemma. For example, I don't really want my tax dollars going to take care of those inmates who are violent and heinous. But it devastates me to watch you experience the harsh reality of prison as a nonviolent offender.

I remember taking you to visit a jail on two occasions—once when you were nine and another time when you were a young teenager. I pleaded with the officers to help you understand about jail and crime. I asked them to scare you, to show you how bad jail would be. They gave you a tour of the jail, but I suspected my efforts had been wasted. They did absolutely nothing to get the point across to you. What could they have done? It was like watching a ticking time bomb. You remember how it was, don't you? When you set your mind to do something, nobody could stop you.

It started when you were just a tike playing your Gameboy. I woke up one night and saw a light glowing from under the door of the closet where we kept the gaming system. I thought the light had been left on by accident, but when I opened the door, there you were on the floor of the closet, playing your little heart out. You just wanted to live life fully on your own terms. And I could not blame you because I wanted the same thing for myself. In fact, I tried to allow you all the freedom I could within the limits of what I thought best for you. You wanted to be right in the middle of whatever you could, experiencing life. And despite all the efforts I had made to prepare myself for motherhood, I felt inadequate much of the time. But for better or worse, I found myself mothering two little boys, wishing I could do it perfectly and knowing that I could not.

After speaking with you yesterday, I got to thinking about

our writing because you told me how you are enjoying the book I sent most recently. You told me that you have been taking some notes about the story you want to write one day. I thought about how far we have come in writing our letters and collaborating on this book. It has been an interesting journey, full of life lessons and time well spent—together. We have spread our wings over the vastness of a great divide, stretched and tempered our fledgling wings, and calmed our anxious hearts with conversation, hugs, prayers, and smiles. We have cried together and comforted each other in the space between bondage and freedom.

When you were a teenager, some of the doctors we consulted theorized that you had not properly bonded during infancy. But when I thought about all the times I held you close to my heart and sang "Lavender's Blue," I knew that was not true. The vivid memory of my pounding heart against your tiny, warm body assured me that our connection was strong and real. Each time I rocked you, I vowed to hold the moments in my heart forever. And I should have known that if we were to be king and queen, like the song said, we would have a few battles.

But we keep rooting each other on in agreement about making this all count. And even though we still have a ways to go, I can see the sun glowing over the distant horizon. I will rise when it rises and rest when it sets—and keep working toward our vision. With arms outstretched, I will dance in the rain whenever it falls and splash in the puddles that remain. We belong somewhere in this great big world of wonder, my son. You are a precious treasure, and I love you all the way to some other world far away—and back again. Furthermore, if I had it to do all over again, I would still choose to have you as my son.

Now, it is time for you to write the story you have been dreaming about. I will tell you, from experience, that you will always believe you need to learn a little more, live a little more, and know a little more.

But I say don't wait.

Write the story now, and write another one later—when you know more. And so on, as many times as you wish. Meanwhile, I will be checking the mail and expecting to read about some fine adventure.

Love,
Mom

~

If you chase two rabbits, you will not catch either one.—Russian proverb

September 28, 2019

Dear Simms,

I have been typing your letters and attempting to put our story together—determined. When I opened this letter to begin typing, I read over a page of notes you sent for future writing. The above quote was scribbled at the corner of a page, and it caught my eye. We have spoken about it before, but I thought it worth another ponder. I would say we finally got settled on one rabbit with this book, and I am hard on his tail with my net. Let's both remember it as we go into our next writing venture. Let's make our focus razor sharp and go after something—anything. Let's go after it until we catch it, no matter what insecurities or distractions come along. If we get another idea, we make a note and keep working until we catch the rabbit we are chasing. After all, no one ever said we can't catch more than one rabbit. We just have to chase them one at a time.

Love,
Mom

~

October 1, 2019

Dear Simms,

I just returned home from visiting a dear friend who is also affected by the opioid crisis. She has a twenty-something-year-old daughter still living at home. The daughter has a son who is toddler age. The grandparents (my friend and her husband) both feel overwhelmed, frustrated, trapped, and exhausted by the circumstances. Most of all, they feel helpless to change it. Their attachment to and concern for their grandchild exacerbate feelings of bewilderment and hopelessness. Feeling the pain of so many others affected by opioid addiction, I am inspired anew to continue working on this project in hopes that it can encourage someone else—or at least offer some measure of comfort.

Love,

Mom

≈

October 3, 2019

Dear Simms,

I saw the little black kitty yesterday, the feral cat who hunts in my yard. It was a comfort to see her, as I feel a little lonely these days. You know that kind of loneliness when you just know this is the way life is? It's not really a bad thing because I could certainly be less alone by participating more in the world around me. However, I enjoy, and seem to need at times, the freedom to create without the constraints that often accompany that participation. Right now, I have to remain focused on finishing this book for the sake of our family, for the sake of my sanity, and for the sake of whatever this book means for humanity.

Do I believe this book is going to change the world, save a soul, or help someone in a way that nothing else can? No. I just want it to be an authentic portrayal of human experience. I feel the end of the project coming like a deep, red horizon across a vast valley. I stand on the precipice knowing I can get there, knowing I am closer than ever before, knowing I have to be brave and share our story, despite inevitable criticism and vulnerability. Also, I feel the good feeling, the excited, hopeful feeling that our diligence has produced a story worth reading. I remind myself that, according to Ralph Waldo Emerson, its effect will be measured "by the depth of sentiment from which it proceeds."

With fondness and love,
Mom

~

October 19, 2019

Today, Simms's energy vibrated through the phone as he told me all about Kairos, a prison ministry group that visited Pender Correctional Center. He had put his name in a bucket for a drawing and got chosen to take part in the program. As a result, he went to the gym all day for singing, eating, and other activities provided by the organization.

"It was tiring but awesome to have a break in the monotony," Simms said. "And I got to eat Bojangles food!"

At the event, Simms also recognized two of the volunteers from a job where he had worked as an assistant to an electrician. They remembered him too, which excited him.

"Seeing them made my day," Simms yelped into the phone, and it soothed my heart to hear his good news.

~

October 30, 2019

Dear Simms,

Your friend Mike, from Wilmington, sent me a message

asking about you. He said he had not heard from you in a while. I told him it had also been a while for me. But you finally called the day before yesterday. I wondered why you did not call for so long, but you said the phones are pretty tied up there. You seemed distracted and spoke to a couple of people while you were on the phone with me. Mike wonders if you are pulling yourself into your environment, closing out the world beyond prison. He said that is something people do as a coping mechanism.

I miss writing to you as I try to finish the book. And I imagine what it will be like when you are free again. An ocean of emotion rises like the tide into my eyes, prompting me to inhale deeply and try to swallow it down. I visualize you on top of a mountain with your bow and arrow. Standing tall and straight, you pull back and aim. Your shoulders and back are bare, lean, and strong. You release, and we watch the arrow hit its target, dead on. I am not surprised. You are an excellent sportsman. I remember watching you with your father shooting skeet, another thing you are good at. I am glad you shared some sporting moments with your dad. Maybe you will write to me about memories of hunting and sporting with Rhett and your dad, since I wasn't usually there for those occasions. I remember going out toward Whiteville once to a skeet-shooting range with all of you. My heart was always happy to see your father teaching you about things he loved. Of course, we all wish there was more of that, but I am grateful for every moment we had. Each one is a treasure nestled forever in my heart.

There was another overdose this week in Morganton—a very nice family. Did I ever tell you about my friend Kathi? Her son was twenty-three when he died from methadone complications. There are so many people struggling with these issues right now. And I have met many of them. One young man is about your age. He has been in recovery ever since I moved here in 2016, and it seems like he is doing well. He uses Subutex. When I asked him about his progress, he explained that he has challenges with anxiety. He is working with an attorney, trying to qualify for disability. This raises more questions in my mind.

With much emotion,

Mom

November 2019

Dear Mom,

It is such a blessing to have you in my life. I cannot thank you enough for always being there for me. You always know what to say. I can't do anything about Dad being gone, but I will make the most of you being here. Lately, my life has been a mess, but you help me stay centered. You give me somewhere to look when I am lost. You are the best role model I could ask for. You motivate me and make me want to succeed —and make it seem possible. Dad would be so proud! Every day, I aspire to be more like you. The passion for reading and writing that you instilled in me will last a lifetime. And right now, it has given me direction and purpose—and that is priceless!

We are going to do great things, Mom. Thanks for everything, from the bottom of my heart. It will all be worth it.

Love always and forever,

Simms

November 2019

Dear Mom,

I just got your last set of letters. Sure do appreciate it! They were all great letters—the set that had the Russian proverb about chasing two rabbits… What an excellent proverb! The letters really made me miss you and Rhett. Plus, the weather is getting cold, and I feel the holidays in the air.

Some people do not like this time of year, but I love it— when I am free. It's a time when I cherish my family and relationships. I know how you feel when you say you sometimes feel lonely, and that is the way life is. I feel that way often. But before I was locked up again, I thought I was past it. I felt so much love from all around me—so close to my family. But now, I feel the loneliness—dark and heavy. Every time I feel the cold, crisp air with no wind, it takes me back to the winter holidays with you and Dad—days of squirrel hunting and cooking squirrel stew on Thanksgiving. It makes me feel like I'm missing a piece of myself without having Dad, and being away from you and Rhett during the holidays…

You could not be better to us, Mom—truly. You are a loving family member who wants the best for us, same as me. I know that no one will ever love me like you, and no one can replace you. You make my life so much richer! It's not fair to any of us that our family cannot be together for the holidays. I am sorry about this. It's my fault. I know I can bring us all together when I get home. I am doing my best in here, but it takes so much out of me. It's lonely here too. Prison makes bad people out of good ones because it doesn't pay to be good in here. Almost all the people I want to respect and trust are only trustworthy sometimes. I'm sick of being a victim in here. I can't just talk to no one and mind my own business, even if I want to do that. People get all up in your business, talk to you, touch your stuff, ask for things. Goddamn gangs give me hell. Had to fight yesterday. Two guys said they wanted to use my radio.

I said, "No, I'm using it."

They said, "Fuck you. You can't say no to us because we are in a gang—and since you tried to stand up for yourself, we are gonna take it and not give it back."

So, I didn't give it up, and they cornered me and yelled and hit me. I kept not hitting back, because it would make it worse. And I didn't want to go to solitary confinement and lose canteen, visits, and calls. I hoped the cops would stop it, but they never did.

The guys went to whoopin' me—and to all the guys who are supposed to be my friends, the gangs said, "Get out of the way! Don't help him!"

And they all listened. They walked away like it was none of their business—one guy who has been helping them, and three who are getting extorted. The gang laughed and called them bitches, and it was true—they were bitches. So, I fought. But in the end, it was pointless because they way outnumbered me. I knew they'd just take the rest of my stuff if I kept fighting, so I had to give it up. Finally, they let me keep the radio, because of something I did. But now, they will expect me to do them whatever favors they want—just for getting to keep what was already mine! I had to give them food, and they said they will pay it back, but that's a lie. They never pay it back!

At least the gang members stick up for each other. They never have to be on their own, and no one messes with them because they know they are not alone. What's more, they get tons of free stuff from extorting people.

Prison will make you sick of being a victim to the point that it's better to hurt other people. And for some reason, I never see other people go through this bullshit! It's always me the gangs want to give a hard time. It has hurt me so much inside. It makes me want to see other people robbed, beat up, and miserable— because misery loves company. I guess I just want other people to hurt as badly as I do. I hope this place doesn't change me forever. Sure do miss the guy I used to be, before all this. He was so much happier.

Sorry to bring you down with such negative stories, but it's heavy on my heart right now. Love you so much, Mom. You don't deserve to feel alone. I just want to hug you and tell you how much you mean to me—remind you how you do things for us that no one else ever will. I understand and share your concerns about other family members and hope things improve. I love you to the end of everything and back, Mom. You are the most priceless thing in my life, and I can't imagine it without you. Thank you for the letter. I will send you some writing soon.

Also, I've been talking to Dom, and she said, "Hey." She wishes you well.

Love forever and always,
Simms

CHAPTER 24

November 17, 2019

Dear Simms,

I dreamed about you a couple of nights ago. You were in prison, but somehow, you got a home-visit pass. We went on an adventure to an amusement park and rode a roller coaster like the Griffin. Remember that time we went to Busch Gardens and rode the roller coaster over and over until the park closed? You rode it alone at first. Then, I decided to ride with you. I wanted to share the fun with you, but I couldn't figure out how to enjoy the ride. It made my stomach all queasy, and I got so tense that I gave myself a migraine. Determined to learn how to enjoy the ride so that we could share special memories of the event, I reasoned for a while and came up with a plan.

As I reflected on my experience with the previous ride, I realized that my discomfort was a result of my resistance to the experience. I decided to try riding with a new mindset. I would sit in the front and pretend I was driving. I would press my foot to the floor, trying to go faster, trying to outrun the coaster. I would dive to the ground on the ten-story drop, instead of falling like I had before. I would head for the ground before the coaster released for the drop.

Sure enough, when I imagined myself ahead of the roller coaster, trying with all my might to stay ahead of it, there was no time to be afraid, no time to resist. There was only time to feel the power of my newfound superhero abilities. I could fly! I could dive to the ground without injury! I could race down the tracks like lightning!

What an amazing experience it was to ride with you on that roller coaster over and over. I will never forget your smile, your enthusiasm for the adventure, our shared laughter as we ran back through a maze of bars, trying to reach the entrance again before the next start. Out of breath, giggling with excitement, and full of energy, we climbed into the coaster again and again, solidifying an extraordinary memory of shared adventure. That night, I left the park completely exhausted—and completely alive.

Thank you for being in my life. Loving you adds a unique and precious facet to my existence—one for which I am immensely grateful.

Love,
Mom

November 22, 2019

I am at Grind Cafe this morning, and the coffee club just arrived. I expressed my condolences to an acquaintance who recently lost his son as a result of an overdose. I feel empathy for his loss—and for the pain he must have experienced before the loss. I imagine the pain he feels now and pray I will never know it.

It has been a few weeks since I saw Simms. And when I don't see him for a while, the empathy I feel for him gets overwhelming. I booked a last-minute flight to Wilmington for a visit. I have to call twenty-four hours in advance to make an appointment for visitation, but I can only call Monday through

Thursday. I got up and headed to the airport early, hoping to get on the first flight. After a whirlwind of activity, I boarded the plane and called to schedule a visit, having forgotten to do it at the airport before boarding.

When I spoke to the visitation officer, he said that Simms was unavailable for visitation. I panicked and said that I was already on a flight to see him, adding that I was his mother. The officer told me to hold on. I told him that I might get cut off, and that I definitely wanted to be scheduled. Then, the flight attendant made me hang up because we were pushing back, preparing for take-off. Why was he unavailable for visitation? Had he been sent to solitary? Was he in the hospital? What happened? My heart did its usual pounding. My gut churned, and my palms were clammy with sweat.

Oh, God, please…

After two hours of trying to calm myself down, telling myself that everything was fine, I landed in Wilmington and called the visitation office again. It was ten minutes past the twenty-four-hour requirement for the 11:15 a.m. visit, so I could not get an extended visit. I took the 2:15 p.m., thankful that he was now miraculously available for visitation and relieved that he must be okay. Meanwhile, all the cortisol in my system had gone straight to my chin, as it erupted in a new patch of stress acne.

The next day, I pulled into the parking lot of Pender Correctional Center. Simms had called the night before to apologize ahead of time for coming to the visitation without a shower. He said the sewer was backed up into the water lines, preventing them from showering or drinking the water for over a week. When he told me that, I could not help but wonder if that was the initial reason they told me he would be unavailable for a visit.

I went to the waiting area and joined a few other people in a row of cold seats along the wall in a narrow concrete hallway. The officer checked my ID, and we all followed him through a door into a courtyard. We crossed the small outdoor area and made a line as instructed. There were four of us, so we were all allowed in together. Usually, it's three at a time for processing. The round, dark woman did not smile. She spoke gruffly, as if we had committed a crime ourselves for daring to visit an inmate.

"Take off your shoes," she said. "Put your keys and ID in here." She shoved plastic containers forward on a table. "You can't have that," she spouted, pointing to a small, transparent pouch the woman ahead of me carried over her shoulder.

"I have a doctor's note in here," she said politely. "This is for my diabetes."

"Well, I don't know about that. You can't have that candy," the guard said. A bag of Skittles exposed itself willingly to the guard's scrutiny. "I'll have to call somebody."

We all waited patiently, barely breathing, ashamed of some crime we hadn't committed, despised by her accusing glare. After much drama with turning pockets inside out and going through a series of detectors, pat-downs, and more harsh instructions about not touching our stuff until permission was granted, we finally exited the building into another courtyard. We waited for the guard who had greeted us initially in the hallway. Then, we followed him into the visitation area.

This facility's visitation room was significantly smaller than all the others I had visited. There were only about ten tables, compared to about sixty or more in the other places. At Mountain View, there are no tables at all. Instead, there are chairs facing each other with tape indicating how close the chairs can be. The space between is just far enough that you have to reach out and bend over to hold hands, making anything other than brief contact unsustainable.

As we entered, I saw a second guard seated on a raised platform behind a computer. Our escort directed me to table number four. The tables are square with wooden blocks in the middle, where the numbers are painted in red. Simms was waiting for me. It had been almost a year since he was transferred from county jail to prison. And this was the only time he had been waiting for me.

The guard who escorted us took his place behind a second computer on the platform. They monitored the visit from behind a chest-high wall, one eating a snack, the other working diligently on some computer task, both staring at their computers, scanning the room occasionally, and commenting to each other in barely audible voices.

"Hi, Mom," Simms pulled me close in a loving embrace as I tiptoed and wrapped my arms around his shoulders.

We hugged for as long as I believed the guards would tolerate. I put my hands on his hair, then reached over his back, feeling his broad shoulders. I kissed his cheek and let my hands fall down along his arms as I backed away to inspect him. He was clean, which I did not expect.

"They finally let me take a shower," he told me, as if he could read my thoughts.

"That's nice!" I said with a smile, trying to get things started in a positive tone. "You look good," I added, taking my seat across the table from him.

I noticed the metal plate embedded on the table before him. I focused on reading the upside-down letters that spelled *inmate*.

"Thanks, Mom. You too."

His words were cordial, but his eyes were dull and lifeless. He took in a deep breath and pushed his lips into an unconvincing smile. With only my key fob and ID on the table, we began to talk, looking directly into each other's eyes, letting ourselves relax into whatever conversation came. I found out that the gangs were still a continual and exhausting presence. They would wake him from his sleep, take his possessions, and show aggression if he resisted their demands.

"It's humiliating, and the guards ignore everything. They just let the gang members extort whoever they want," Simms said under furrowed brows. I stared at the dark circles under his bloodshot eyes and felt a sharp pain in my heart. "If I report the extortion, they will put me in solitary, which is the most miserable existence of all," he continued as his head shook back and forth over slumped shoulders.

In our face-to-face visits, we could talk about everything without being audio recorded. Of course, we talked quietly. But at least I could get the truth of what was going on. He told me about the availability of drugs within the system. Inmates could buy legal, nonprescription medication from a weekly cart that offered snacks and necessities like toothpaste and soap. Many inmates continued feeding their drug habits using meth, heroin, or pills. I learned through conversations with other visitors that drugs entered the prison most often through bodily cavity transport. The drugs were then exchanged during visitation.

"How is your spiritual state?" I asked, not knowing anything else to say after he updated me on his state of affairs.

"Nonexistent," he said. "How can God do this to me? I just can't think about it at all. If I do, the anger just rages inside me. I just can't understand how God can let me suffer like this."

I listened, then reached across the table toward him. Squeezing his hands, I looked into his eyes and waited for him to continue. His eyelids drooped over deep blue-gray irises. I looked at his brown curls and thought about how they had grown so much since he had to shave them. His hair was a puffy array of shiny tendrils, bouncy and hopeful, contrasting with the despair that dripped from his face.

"Your hair is getting long," I said, hoping to lighten the mood. "Do you have conditioner?"

"Yeah," he said, "but no comb. I use my fingers, but I'll

probably have to cut it again before long. I don't think I can manage it much longer—I mean, I hope I can keep it. I miss it being long."

"You know I love your hair—so beautiful, like your dad's." I smiled and looked at him with endearment, seeing his father in him and feeling the warmth of our togetherness, our mutual fondness for the formidable spirit of his dad. "Tell me about the story you're writing," I went on.

His eyes brightened for a moment, and he relayed some details about the characters and plot. "The dialogue is hard, though. I get stuck, and end up summarizing what's happening, putting off the dialogue," he said.

"Yes, I tended to do that in the drafting of my novel. I avoided the dialogue. Now, I wish I had worked on it as I went along."

I told him what I had been learning about dialogue—how it can move the story along, how the pace can be affected by the white space. I heard myself getting too far into instruction and sensed I was losing him to the reality of his circumstances. I recognized his efforts to engage with me, but survival, discomfort, and the obstacles of imprisonment were taking their toll on his mental state, threatening to seize him, clawing at his sanity, stripping his motivation, eroding his attention with the torturous drip, drip, dripping of time.

My mind flashed back to Europe, where I was alone in my travels. I saw myself on the streets of Naples, beggars and predators lining the streets, waiting to seize their prey with the first sign of distraction or inattention. I thought about how it might feel to exist in a constant state of vulnerability for such a prolonged period. My heart sank with sadness for him, hoping I could somehow keep the flame of hope alive for him so that he could keep moving. I saw us in a snowstorm, cold and lost. I was trying to keep his spirit warm long enough for salvation to come.

Please, God, help us. Please don't let him die. Please don't let them kill his spirit. Thank You for Your grace, Your comfort, for life and love, for our time together. Please, God, let him feel Your love. Teach him what he needs to know. Guide him toward life.

My heart prayed as I watched Simms through glossy eyes. With a blink, tears rolled down my cheeks, and I let the silence tell him all my heart was saying.

Our wandering minds took us into topics of food, sleep, family, pen pals, his instructors, and holidays, among other things. He was in such a state of misery over his current situation with the gangs that he was ready to leave the program and give up whatever time he could earn off his sentence. It had become unbearable.

"I might talk to my instructor to see if I can leave the program early. I just can't take it anymore. I don't get any sleep, and it's a constant shakedown. The police don't do anything except trash my stuff and write me up for whatever they can. They wrote me up for having a lock that wasn't on my locker. Oh, and how long has it been since you mailed the letters to India and Japan?" he asked.

"Hmmm. I think I mailed them as soon as I got them from you. I can't remember, though. I'll check at home to make sure they are not in with your other letters. Surely, I mailed them right away," I said in my best reassuring tone.

Eventually, the guards announced that visitation was over. We hugged again until they made a final declaration in a stern voice. I kissed him and gave his curls a quick swipe.

"I love you, Simms. Hang in there," I said.

"Love you too, Mom. You're the best. Thanks for everything."

I swallowed hard as I walked back through the exits toward the parking lot, pushing the pain back into its place at the bottom of my heart. It resisted as I tried to lock it away.

I have to smile. I have to live a happy life. Somebody has to do it. I have to let myself be happy. I tried to remind myself that it was okay for me to have fun and enjoy my life. But how? I didn't find the answer to that question that day, or the day after, or the day after that. But I promised myself I would not stop trying.

My mind wandered back over the years to several times when Simms was sick and throwing up. I asked why, but he closed me out. Despite my prodding, I could not get him to look me in the eyes and talk to me. I remember when he burned his foot and received other injuries. When I discovered his burned foot, I took him to the doctor, concerned that he might lose his foot. He was limping and not wearing a shoe because his foot had swollen so much that he could not fit it into a shoe. He resisted my taking him to the doctor with his irritability and refusal to go. Then, he wouldn't open up about what had happened, about how he had been injured. I wondered why he kept hurting himself, wondered if he was doing it on purpose—even though he said he wasn't. Nevertheless, he would get upset and defensive anytime I pried or questioned him about what was happening.

"Why are you hurting yourself?" I asked him. "I want to help you. Please help me understand. I love you."

"I'm not doing it on purpose! It was a freaking accident!" he yelled, turning from me, resisting, closing himself, reminding me of his father.

Ben was a private man. Furthermore, he didn't want a counselor, a wife, or even a friend telling him how to live his life, even if it may have improved something. He'd rather pay the price and have the freedom to do as he pleased, even if it wasn't what anyone else thought was right, even if he didn't think it was optimal himself. It was his deal, and that was the end of it. Early on, it was obvious that Simms had this independent spirit too. And he got it rightfully from both sides. I like the freedom to be my own person. Or, as Emerson would suggest, I live by my own constitution.

Because of my personal desire for autonomy, I respected Ben and my sons in this regard. I tried to balance parental guidance with the understanding of how it felt to be controlled as a child. I can say for certain that I rushed my childhood away, but unlike others who have done that and talked about it, I don't regret it. I was ready to be an adult, to be free, to make my own mistakes and pay the consequences. I just wanted to live as most of us do —freely. I believe I would rather die than be controlled. So, how can I be angry at my son for insisting on doing things his own way? I did try to stop him from hurting himself as much as I knew how. I did the best I could, made every effort to help him see the best way, to protect him. However, he was always strong-willed. He bucked and bucked, and he wasn't going to stop bucking. He had to do it his way, and now, he's paying some heavy consequences. I love him, and I still imagine the best for him. Every beat of my heart prays that he will have a joyful and peaceful life, one full of extraordinary wonder and delight.

But if my son was asking me to suffer his consequences for him or expecting financial support, I would need to recognize my option to do what is best for my own situation. I would have to remember I do not owe that to him or anyone else. If he was blaming everyone else for his circumstances and not taking responsibility for his actions, I would have to wait until he was ready to take personal responsibility for his circumstances before I could engage fully in the process of connecting with him to build the trust required for genuine intimacy and functional family relations.

Before Simms went to jail, he worked very hard at participating in a rehabilitation program. I could see that he was trying with all his might to live a good, clean life. By the same token, I could also see when he slipped. I had concerns for his safety and the ultimate outcome of his life. However, I knew he had to find his path. And my role as the parent of a young adult would be different. I would love him and make regular efforts to remain connected through visits and correspondence. I would offer encouragement and give opinions when asked. The rest would be up to him.

PART III

Fear

You lurk in the shadows
And stalk me in the dark
Waiting there with jealous fumes
To bite without a bark

Your greedy eyes are piercing
Desperately, they gleam
With a cold, sharp blade you haunt me
Aiming to whittle my dream

Oh, bully with your shining knife
Who do you think I am?
I've learned a thing or two of you
And I say you are damned

You coward, with your veil of lies
I am on a mission
My sword is drawn in ready stance
I've made a firm decision

I'll stop my running, fumbling self
And turn toward your stench
To chase you down and slay you sound
I'll slice you inch by inch

But wait! I lay upon you now
Prepared to pay the price
And find beneath me, nothing there
But an empty shell of ice!

So, now I know the truth of it
My heart is full at last
Waving boldly evermore
Freedom's flag, full mast!

CHAPTER 25

The Prison Transfer

By Simms

It was 2:00 a.m. on December 19, 2019, when a corrections officer shook me awake and handed me two small plastic bags.

"You're shipping out. Get packed up."

I knew it was coming any day, but despite my eagerness to be far away from Pender Correctional Center, I sure did dread the transfer.

As I packed, I prepared myself for one of the most unpleasant experiences of my life. I'm not sure if knowing it would be horrible made it easier or harder—just two sides of a torture chamber, I suppose. My first transfer was more than a year ago, when I went from county jail to Polk Correctional. All I could hope is that it would be better than that one, or any of the others since then. Hope for the best, prepare for the worst. Right?

First, all the relocating prisoners carried our property to the front of the prison where we would get on the bus. There, we proceeded to unpack our stuff again for another search of our belongings and person. The clothes I was wearing joined a heap of belongings on the floor as I forced my mind elsewhere to avoid the demeaning process of comprehensive bodily inspection. An hour or so later, that part of the nightmare was over. Breakfast was a carton of milk, an apple, and a bologna sandwich.

Then, we waited a couple more hours until almost daybreak, 5:00 or 5:30 a.m. When we finally boarded the bus, it was a relief to get moving, but it was bittersweet because the prison had taken our jackets and any nonessential clothing. It was December 19 and freezing cold. We were transported into a modified school bus with bars on the windows, a metal partition between us and the driver, and a back emergency door modified for entry and exit of prisoners.

Of course, the bus was painted the favorite color of the American prison system—beige, which I now believe must be the color of hell. To our dismay, the bus had no heat or air conditioning. I had hoped to go back to sleep on the bus, as I was exhausted from being up since 2:00 a.m., but alas, it was not meant to be. At the time, I believed that I had never been so cold in my life, and my uncontrollable shivering kept me awake the duration of the trip.

We traveled around, picking up inmates from other prisons in a haphazard manner that had no consideration for efficiency, going forty-five minutes past one prison to another only to reverse direction and return to the first prison we had passed. Before long, the bus was crowded to full capacity, preventing us from lying down or achieving any sort of comfort for the remainder of our eighteen-hour bus ride.

At about 10:00 am, we arrived at a prison transportation hub called Sandy Ridge, a bus depot with barbed-wire fences and gun towers. In the center were two buildings—one for the guards, and one concrete box for prisoners. When our bus arrived there, the driver pulled in and parked. Then, we spent another two hours trapped in the bus.

When we were finally released from the bus, meal two was served in a paper bag—another milk, another apple, and another bologna sandwich. We were herded into the concrete building called the bullpen, which made the overcrowded bus seem like a free fall through space. Hundreds of prisoners were crammed shoulder to shoulder in the open holding pen.

There was a big container with water in it, four toilets out in the open, and a dehumanizing lack of privacy—so nothing new. Prisoners with drugs or tobacco worked their way to the back to sell it for stamps, or to smoke in the crowded holding pen. Gang members met each other, and prisoners exchanged information about different prisons. We spent an hour or two packed in the bullpen like cattle. Then, the guards began to call our names over the intercom. The officers never entered the bullpen, so drug use and violence were not suppressed.

It was a relief to get back on the bus again, around 1:00 or 2:00 p.m. We were searched again before getting on the next bus to complete the last leg of the tedious journey. We continued making rounds to prisons all over the state, picking up people and taking them to other prisons. Of course, my destination was the last stop! By the time we approached Mountain View Correctional Institution, it was pitch dark outside.

There were no stops for bathroom breaks on these bus rides. Instead, one of the seats had been removed. In its place was a large steel box with a hole in the middle. There were no walls for privacy, and I was disgusted. I went to the back to use the makeshift toilet as we were driving up a curvy mountain road. It was so dark that I could not see my feet. The bus was so crowded, and I had to climb over seats and people. The curves continued to throw me off my feet as I attempted to relieve myself. I could barely stand, let alone hit the target or allow my bladder to relax and empty. And with six people within arm's reach of me, I was beyond uncomfortable. I pushed my way through the excruciating ordeal and felt like I had accomplished a feat nothing short of Mount Everest!

Finally, we arrived at Mountain View around 8:00 p.m. My

eighteen-hour journey was almost over. As we pulled into the unloading bay, a gang member in solitary confinement asked if any of his people were on the bus. We exited the bus and went inside, where we were handed our last meal of the journey. You guessed it—milk, an apple, and a bologna sandwich! We were strip searched again and had our property searched thoroughly—again. The officers gave us hell and threw away everything they possibly could. Then, they sent us to get medical examinations before admittance into the housing unit. Finally, at 10:00 p.m., I lay down to sleep, feeling barely alive and most certainly not human.

February 7, 2020

Yesterday, a big storm came. After hours of heavy rainfall, I smelled something burning. It smelled like melting plastic, so I thought it must be electrical. I bolted down the stairs and pounded on the door to Rhett's unit.

With adrenaline surging, I yelled, "What's burning?" through the locked door that connected the two units internally.

"I don't know!" Rhett's girlfriend yelled back, matching my frantic tone.

I ran around to the front door, which she had already opened, and darted inside. Rushing from one room to the next with my senses on high alert, I searched for the smell, trying to determine the level of our emergency. It was strong throughout the house, feeding my panic. When I reached the dining room, my head was spinning, thinking, working, and I realized the smell was strongest there, above the basement. Everything came together in my mind. The basement must have flooded, shorting out the furnace. I darted out the back door to the basement entrance behind the house and saw it about three feet deep in water. I couldn't get to the electric panel to turn off the breaker switch without going through deep water that might be electrically charged, so I called 911.

Emergency crews arrived in record time. Within minutes, fire trucks and public safety vehicles lined my street. A feeling of pride came over me as I watched the firefighters and public safety officers handle the situation. They went through the house to make sure no fires were active and respectfully asked me to stay out of the house until they could be sure it was safe. Then, they offered suggestions for managing the aftermath, with consideration for limited resources. An hour or so later, we had no electricity, no gas, no heat, and no hot water. But we were safe, with a roof over our heads.

I learned a lot about the importance of a properly functioning sump pump that day. Even though it's a small, relatively inexpensive bit of equipment, it deserves regular attention and maintenance as it protects more expensive items like the furnace from potential water damage. I never knew how much the sump pump worked down there. It wasn't just pumping out a little water here and there. That baby was working overtime!

The firefighters told me that getting the water drained quickly could minimize the damage to the unit. First, I tried to get the old sump pump to work, but it wouldn't budge. So, I went to the home improvement store and bought a new one. A few hours later, after much ado trying to get the new pump up and running, the basement was dry. During the rigmarole, I set up appointments for technicians to get things back in working order. The hot water heater was ruined, so I had to get a plumber to install a new one. When he arrived, he turned on the electricity and gas. To my relief and amazement, the furnace fired up with no hesitation! I cheered and jumped around with grateful abandon over my good fortune. The possibility of major repairs on the furnace was heavy on my mind as I scolded myself for being ignorant about the sump pump. It had been a bit temperamental a few times, so I should have known better than to continue relying on it. But, as I stated earlier, I just did not realize the work it was actually doing during rainstorms.

After getting things back in relative order, my panic resolved into emotion as I thought of all the years I didn't have to face emergencies with all the responsibility on my own shoulders. Missing Ben, I stirred the pot of sentiments simmering on my soul until it turned to gratitude for my ability to solve problems and take care of myself. Then, I wrapped myself in one of Ben's old shirts and imagined him hugging me with pride. I felt so alone and wondered if I would ever get used to being just me.

> *Sometimes,*
> *I try to be strong.*
> *I tell myself I will be strong.*
> *I go through the strong motions.*
> *I work and smile and say,*
> *"I'm fine, thank you,"*
> *Or, "Yes, all is well."*

> *Sometimes,*
> *I want someone else,*
> *To be the strong one,*
> *To go through the strong motions,*
> *To hold me close and say,*
> *"You are safe and warm,"*
> *Or, "Everything is okay."*

February 17, 2020

I visited Simms at Mountain View Correctional Institute on Sunday, and he had somewhat recovered emotionally from a write-up he had received for accepting a cookie from another inmate. The offense would add time to his sentence, so he pleaded with the guards and tried to explain his innocence. But the guards used the incident for entertainment and teased him about it while he grieved the extension of his sentence.

"Now, I might not get out this year at all!" he said over the phone when he told me about the ordeal.

However, by the time I saw him, they had reconsidered his case and deferred the charges.

Having reclaimed some positive energy before our visit, Simms shared much about the writing he had been doing lately. He sat strong in his chair as he talked about things he had learned from reading and thinking. And his authentic, warm manner expressed passion for his ideas and conclusions. Sincerity beamed from his eyes, and I could feel hope nestling itself between us like a newborn pup. I was comforted by our togetherness. When we sat facing each other in that cold cinderblock room, there was something that mattered—our genuine connection, our hopes and dreams, and the sound of our voices singing together about life and its meaning for us. With the color of hell all around us, we made the best of our visit and drummed up some joy.

CHAPTER 26

March 8, 2020

I surprised Simms for a visit on Ben's birthday. Simms had called the day before to tell me about a violent encounter he had with another inmate. For this reason, I was eager to assess his condition in person. The clocks moved forward that day for Daylight Savings, so it was dark when I set out for Spruce Pine, the location of Mountain View Correctional Institute. I bathed myself in fond memories of Ben to honor his birthday as I drove along a scenic route we had taken on the motorcycle many times. And I thanked God that Simms had survived yet another dangerous event with his life and faculties intact.

When Simms told me the story on the phone, I wished I could have recorded it. He told it with just the right details, sentiments, and emotion.

"You have a true gift of sharing your stories," I said. "I am so proud of you, Simms."

My eyes grew moist as I imagined his physical pain and heard the pride in his voice when he told me how he stood up to the bully who tried to take advantage of him.

At the start of our contact visit, I asked him to tell me all about the fight again—from the beginning, so I could understand it all and write about it. First, he reminded me about his roommate who stayed up all night.

"Why does he stay up all night?" I asked. "Is he on drugs?"

"Yeah."

"Was it heroin, or what?"

"Uppers," he said as he shifted a long strand of curls hanging in front of his eye, slowly placing it behind his ear so that I barely noticed the gesture at all.

His eyes shone brightly over two boats of yellow skin shadowed with dark settlements of old blood. The swelling and initial purple bruising that would have been present earlier had subsided, I noted.

"So, when did the incident happen?" I asked, leaning toward him.

The chairs were about five feet apart, so it was difficult to hear with the thirty or so other families visiting in the spacious cement room with rows of plastic chairs. Some of the other institutions had tables in the visitation rooms, but Mountain View had only chairs. Rows facing the visitor entrance were designated for visitors and indicated by gray chairs. Facing the opposite direction, inmates sat in beige chairs.

"Wednesday afternoon, after chow," he answered.

His eyes scanned the room as he leaned back briefly in his chair and shrugged one shoulder to adjust the gray t-shirt hanging there. His hands slid slowly over his thighs, smoothing the beige fabric of his pants from hip to knee, while his eyes remained sharp and proud. I watched the steady rise and fall of his chest. He was calmer than I had seen him in a long time. I watched him tell the story, seeing how it had affected him in a positive way.

"So, who was the guy?" I asked. "Did he just come in and start giving you a hard time?"

"Well, it started when my cellmate—let's call him Lou—got hold of some meth. He started spending his own money on drugs and following me to the canteen for a handout. Lou started in with, 'Awe, man, you gettin' us some drink mix, right?' And I said, 'No, man!' But he kept it up. 'Dude! That is so nice of you, man. Thank you. I been needin' some drink mix. Man, that's gonna be good!' I said, 'You must have misunderstood. I told you, no. I'm not gettin' you any drink mix.' He said, 'Whaat?! Naw, man. That ain't right. Why you bein' all stingy like that, man?' I told him, 'You have money. Get your own drink mix.' So, he said, 'Awe, naw, man. I can't do that. I just can't do that.' And I knew why. He had to use his money for drugs." Simms moved his fingers lightly across his chin, where a large lesion covered one side.

"How's the pain?" I asked.

"It's okay, except for the mouth pain. I have what feels like fever blisters inside my mouth, behind my lip, and on my tongue. It wakes me up during the night when it gets dry from me breathing with my mouth open while I sleep. The pain is excruciating. They gave me Tylenol when they checked me out after the fall," Simms said, as he raised his brow and pursed his lips to stress the word fall. "But I didn't want to take more of it because it's hard on the liver with hep C."

"Let me see inside your mouth."

He leaned forward and pulled out his lower lip. The lesions were profuse and white with puss. I cringed, imagining his pain and hoping the infection would heal without further complication.

"I think you should request another doctor visit, just to make sure there is no staph infection. Maybe you can get some sort of mouth rinse that can help with healing." We both sat silently for a few moments, as if honoring his pain. "Okay, so your roommate was irritated?" I asked.

"Yeah. Then, he was in line for the phone beside the guy who would later attack me. 'Hey, why don't you give me a phone call?' the attacker guy yelled at me. I said, 'I don't have any money on my phone account.' So, Lou said, 'Dude! He's lyin' to you. He just straight up lied to you, man! He's got money and a locker full of stuff too!' After that, the guy came into my room. 'Yo! Open your locker. I'm takin' your stuff,' he said. I said, 'No, you can't have my stuff.' He said, 'Is that right?' as he came closer. I jumped off my top bunk where I had been reading before he came in. At that moment, I knew I had a big problem because I was in my socks."

Simms pushed himself up in the color-of-hell plastic chair, lifting his shoulders and tilting his head so that a long ringlet of dark brown hair fell to the side of his face. His movements were slow and purposeful, graceful and composed. He showed no sign of discomfort as he told the story, which reminded me of his high tolerance for pain. I watched—amazed—as he proceeded, catering subtly to his mouth as he let the story flow out. His words were concise, and the simple structure of his speech captivated me with the eloquence of a master poet.

"It's a general rule not to be caught without your shoes off, but I was on my bed, so I wanted to relax a little. I was at a real disadvantage without my shoes. Plus, he had about forty pounds on me."

"And then?"

"The extortioner hit me in the mouth as I was saying something to him, and my teeth came down on my lip. Blood started flowing, and he threw his body against me. I fell to the floor and took him with me. We wrestled on the floor until he grabbed my windpipe and squeezed. 'I'll kill you right here!' he yelled. With my air completely closed off, I thought he might accidentally kill me, if not on purpose. I couldn't get any air, so I let go of him. The Muslim prayer leader guy I told you about came to the door of the cell with another guy I don't really know. They told the extortioner to get out, and he did. They brought an ointment to put on my face to stop the bleeding. It helped, but the cut on my nose bled for a long time. Several guys came asking if I was okay, complimenting me on standing up to the bully. There was blood everywhere, so one of my friends used a t-shirt to mop it up. It's like I'm finally respected, and it feels really good."

"So, what happened after things were cleaned up?"

"The bully—I don't know his name, and I think he didn't know mine, either—came up to me and tried to buddy up with me. Said he had my back from now on, or something like that. But I ignored him. The next morning, I went to my horticulture class, as usual, keeping my head down so that my hair would hang in my face."

I looked at Simms's face and imagined how it must have looked three days before. Was the yellow under his eyes normal? I've seen yellow on old bruises before, but I had additional concerns because of our recent conversations about hep C. My heart said a wordless prayer, and I let it go. In this moment of connection, he was okay.

I will not let fear or anxiety about the unknown pollute this moment of togetherness, I thought.

"So, you weren't worried about having the guy in your block? The bad guy?" I asked.

"No, not really. The other guys said they were gonna get him out of there one way or another, but I wasn't thinking about that. I was just hoping to stay out of the hole. Plus, my injuries were enough to keep me in the moment with my mouth on fire, my nose throbbing, and my whole body feeling like it had been run over by a freight train." Simms leaned back in his chair and scanned the room with keen eyes, before stretching his shoulders back and again tucking the errant lock of persistent curls behind his ear.

Those curls, I thought with endearment for him and his father. I had always wanted to see Ben's hair long. In a photo of him as a younger man, it was pulled back into a neat ponytail at the base of his neck, where it fell past his shoulder blades, undetectable. The photo was from before I met him, and despite my encouragement, he never grew it longer than about eight inches during the time I knew him. And with his tight curls, that was just enough to make a big puffy halo around his head.

"So, what happened in horticulture class?"

"Nothing. I kept my head down, and nobody asked me anything."

A noise from behind Simms distracted him, and he turned toward it with a slow, fluid twist of his torso. I was intrigued by the consistent level of coolness he displayed, as I had not witnessed it much prior to his incarceration.

I thought of a time, not long before his latest arrest, when we were hiking Profile Trail to Grandfather Mountain. We wanted to hike the whole trail, but the ranger told us we had to go back because the park was closing. The idea of someone restricting his behavior had always been a trigger. And this time was no exception. An hour later, as we exited the park, I was thanking my lucky stars he had not gotten arrested.

I pulled my attention back to our visit and considered how much he was maturing. *At least he is gleaning something good from his hard times,* I thought. *Can he hold on to love and prevent the system from destroying his core—his soulful inner beauty?* Yes, I thought as I smiled with pride at the man sitting before me. *I believe he can. I have to believe.*

Then, Simms continued, "But when I left class to go back to the block, we all had to get searched. It's standard procedure—I guess to make sure we don't try to bring back garden tools or anything." There was a pause as I watched Simms stare into the distance, searching for his next thought. "That's when a sergeant noticed my face and took me over to the side to ask what happened. I told him I fell off my bunk and hit my face on the table," Simms said, as his shoulders bounced with a chuckle that erupted through a half smile. I smiled back, seeing how his storytelling mannerisms were so much like his father's.

"Did he believe you?" I asked.

"Not likely," Simms said through a widening smile that spread to his eyes. "He just said, 'Well, you're gonna have to go down to medical and get checked out.'" Simms leaned to the other side of his chair and petted the tuft of hair sprouting from his chin. "On the way there, a captain saw me. He stopped me and asked the same thing. 'What happened?' And I repeated what I had already told the sergeant. 'You gotta go to medical,' the captain said, and I told him that's where I was headed—that the sergeant had sent me. Then, the captain said, 'Come on,' and went with me. 'But if that's your story, you better stick to it.'

"Then, the nurse checked me out and asked about my injuries and how they happened. I spit the words out exactly the same, like a recording, and she stared at me. I guess she was waiting for me to cave and tell the truth. I just looked back and waited. After a minute, the captain said, 'You know I don't believe you, right? None of us believe you. The guards don't believe you. The sergeant don't believe you. The nurse don't believe you, and I don't believe you. Are you sure that's what happened?' I said I was sure, so he shrugged and left me there.

"I knew I had to go to solitary for a bit, until they could sort things out and get to the bottom of what really happened, but I knew they couldn't keep me there long because I stuck to my story."

I smiled and stared at him, waiting for more of the story. He took a deep breath.

"After a few hours," he went on, "they sent me back to my cell, and the bad guy was gone. That's all I know about it. The other guys in the block patted me on the back and congratulated me on standing up for myself—for not letting him take my stuff. They told me the guy wasn't coming back. The gang had a beef with him now, and they were on my side—even though I'm not in a gang. They ran him out because he broke gang rules by jumping me like that."

"What rule did he break? Don't gangs extort people?" I asked.

"Some of them do, yeah. But he was messin' in their territory."

"Oh, gotcha," I said. "What happened to him?"

I scooted to the edge of my seat to get closer because we were talking quietly. I straightened my back and stretched my legs. There was no clock in the room, though my eyes scanned it for some idea of how much time we had left—orienting myself to who and what was around us. When Simms and I entered these conversations, it was as if time stood still.

"Well, he was just gone, and the guys told me he wasn't coming back," Simms said.

"I sure am glad you're okay," I said, looking into his dark, clear eyes with overwhelming endearment for the person there—hoping all good things for him, ignoring the tugs of apprehension that tried to squirm into my gut.

I have to appreciate the time we have now, and let tomorrow work itself out, I reminded myself. *There is nothing for me to do with tomorrow. I will let it be a rainbow encircling the sky of a beautiful today. Heaven is the love we share at this moment. Tomorrow will take care of itself.*

After we parted, I resumed my positive affirmations as I followed the majestic curves of Appalachia and let them take me home.

I will prepare for the future in practical ways, but I will not worry about it. I will use my faculties to make it as well as I can. Then, I will embrace today with gratitude. I will live the best I can in the grace of each moment and let wind take up my joy. The seeds of a life well lived will float and scatter, germinate and grow. Peace will rise around me like a mountain spring, and I will drink it like a well-rooted tree. All is well.

After our visit on March 8, North Carolina Division of Prisons suspended civilian visitations because of the COVID-19 virus. The United States, along with many other countries, experienced an economic shutdown as authorities put strict regulations in place to control the spread of the virus. Social distancing and quarantine orders changed the way Americans lived from day to day. During this period of lockdown, I decided to stay with my boyfriend, Grant, near Marshall, North Carolina, until things improved.

Being amid nature on a mountain offered the relief and safety I craved during a time when the whole world seemed like it might fall apart. Additionally, Rhett's hostile actions and negative attitude tainted the positive feelings of love and safety I had previously associated with my home in Morganton. Furthermore, my apprehension was compounded by not being able to visit Simms face-to-face in prison. The drama of my family circumstances stalked me like a beast on the trail of its prey. And all I wanted was to hide in the woods until the monster sated its hunger without me.

Meanwhile, Simms's release was set for September 30, with speculation that some prisoners may be released early because of the global pandemic.

In a conversation with Simms on the phone, he said, "Every day feels like an eternity right now."

And I agreed. We were both a wreck about whether he would make it to release. It was like the last days of a pregnancy when you know the baby is still okay and feel each risky second ticking like a time bomb, threatening to sabotage it all. He was anxious about his release, hoping it would be real, worried that something would prevent it. And our fears were confirmed when his caseworker told him his home plan had been rejected.

We were both concerned. Furthermore, I wanted him to know that I would be there for him, to help him figure things out as he began the next chapter of his life. But I also needed to believe that I was allowed to enjoy my life. And the road I saw ahead of me was not desirable or appealing. How much sacrifice would be enough? I could not forsake my son, no matter how upsetting the alternative. I could not forsake myself, no matter how strong my feelings of obligation toward my family. How would I reconcile these issues? I would have to listen for the still, small voice and gather my mana each day with gratitude—one morsel of wisdom at a time.

Even though I knew this, sadness churned in my stomach for a couple of days. I was frustrated that the officer rejected the home plan without calling me to inquire about the discrepancies, but I understood. The officers had gone to the house to evaluate the proposed home plan and found my niece occupying my upstairs apartment, with Rhett and his girlfriend still residing in the downstairs unit. This raised suspicion that I did not own or have authority over the property in question—or that it, at least, would not be a suitable residence for Simms.

Parole officials took their opportunity to reject having a felon released into their community. And I could not blame them for that. Why would they go the extra mile for me and my family by helping me get my son released into a community they were trying to protect from unlawfulness? It was logical for them to reject it, but I was angry and frustrated that they had not made an appointment to meet me there since I had been willing and waiting for their call. It was yet another reminder Simms had served his prison sentence, but he would experience the consequences of his choices wherever he went—for a long time.

So, I relied on my faith in God for peace and hoped Simms could do the same. I fought the demons who said I was selfish for spending time with Grant in the mountains instead of staying in Morganton.

When I spoke with Simms's caseworker, she told me that his plan would eventually be approved. But this did not help with Simms's concern that it could affect a possible early release. I waited for him to call so that I could tell him he must request a meeting with his caseworker to override the social distancing rules related to her position. She told me she could meet with him only at his request. I believed if they met, he would establish a good rapport and have a better chance of getting out ahead of schedule.

CHAPTER 27

Meanwhile, in April 2020, I took up oil painting, since communities were on lockdown because of the pandemic. I set up a studio in Grant's basement and tried to paint away the condemnation that clawed at me and told me I should have stayed in Morganton instead of spending the lockdown with Grant. Because I was not at my house in Morganton when the officers came to investigate the home plan, they received inaccurate information, which led to the rejection of the plan. Even though I had told the case manager to have them call me so I could meet them at the house, they did not contact me. Therefore, I was not at the house when they came to assess the situation. In my efforts to ward off the guilt that plagued my conscience, I delved into the buttery comfort of oil and pigment, letting the colors tell me what I could not tell myself.

You are allowed to be happy, I told myself. And as my brush moved back and forth over the canvas, I breathed—until the stifling grip of guilt weakened and fell away. My second oil painting, the book cover image, took shape as emotion about a paradox tossed like a stormy sea in my soul.

Simms lives behind bars as a consequence of his crimes, while Rhett walks free with walls and bars around his heart.

Simms counts the days until his release, while Rhett secures his walls and bars.

When Simms gets out of prison, will he find freedom in recovery from addiction? Will Rhett ever tear down the prison he has built around his heart? I pray the answer to both will be yes.

As time passed, the idea of Simms's release took shape as a possible reality. My gut told me that if he was going to make it through probation, Rhett had to move out. Actually, it was more than my gut. It was based on hard facts related to Rhett's behavior. When he did not get his way, things got ugly: broken doors and fixtures, dumped garbage in storage buildings, ketchup and mustard spread over bicycles, household linens thrown out the back window onto the lawn, outdoor water faucets turned on wide open for days at a time while I was out of town, stolen household and personal items, shattered flower pots with live plants in them, and unnecessary confrontations with lawn maintenance crews. Additionally, Rhett had instigated some run-ins with local law enforcement.

It was time to solve some hard problems. I did not want to give up on the idea that Simms could have a fresh start and live a good life without getting into any more trouble with the law. Additionally, I had done my best to be a supportive mother to Rhett during Simms's incarceration in the hopes that he could move through his grief about the loss of his father and begin to make progress. Things had not moved along as I had hoped, and whenever I tried to interact with Rhett, he consistently responded with hostility. I needed him to move out of my house because of his antagonistic manner. After Rhett tried to stop my lawn man from mowing the yard by putting his foot in front of a running lawn mower and making a scene, I reached my wit's end with his disregard for my authority as owner of the property.

When I consulted an attorney about the matter, he advised me to consider selling my home as the easiest way to accomplish an eviction. One part of me was distraught about that idea, but another part of me saw it as permission to escape. So, I latched on to the positive aspects of my circumstances and launched into action. My heart stung from the broken relationship between me and Rhett, but I could not fix it alone. I would have to wait and hope that one day he would be ready to join me in trying to mend what was broken. For the time being, I would keep working on things I had power to change.

When I originally met with the attorney about evicting Rhett and he suggested I needed to sell my home, it was like the universe giving me a ticket to run away from my family gone awry. But love finds its own way around what seems impossible. With bated breath, I hoped Rhett would move out of the house without confrontation. If all went as planned, he would move out before the end of June.

May 9, 2020

Dear Simms,

Yesterday, I spoke with your case manager. Then, I called and left a message with your probation officer in Morganton. Neither your case manager nor I have heard back from him. But I gained more understanding about the home plans and the approval process. In light of what I learned from talking with your case manager, I realized I needed to solve some problems.

As you know, I am planning to sell the house. And even though it may not affect your home plan until it's a done deal, I think we should keep it in mind. This will help us make better arrangements for your long-term success. Asheville has some housing options that might work, and I think it would be a good place to consider. I called some transitional housing programs to learn about their expectations and procedures—even though, in the past, you have not desired to live in a community home. I mention it because there could be some benefits. After all, since you would not be required to live there by court order, you could move to another living situation whenever you want.

Transitional housing offers residents easy access to many community resources like counseling, medication-assisted treatment, group therapy, and even financial support that can help residents prepare for independent living. Additionally, a home plan that has a record of success would appeal to your case manager and the warden because "it minimizes prison liability," according to your caseworker. Those in positions to approve release would appreciate the potential for success in a home plan that includes transitional housing. In other words, the chances of your plan getting approved go up tremendously if you opt for transitional housing. If you choose transitional housing, you will have the time and freedom to explore a new community while living in a socially supportive environment. This could lessen the stress and trauma associated with your release.

If you decide that you would like to explore this option further, give Alvin a call. If y'all hit it off and you agree to comply with program expectations, he says he will approve your transition, and you'll have a new home plan—one that is likely to be approved quickly. Being in a transitional home during the initial stages of your release could reduce scrutiny from law enforcement as well. Your probation officer will probably be much easier to tolerate when you have a support network (or something that appears to be a support network to him and the justice system).

I know it is not appealing to go into a situation with lots of rules and regulations, but I imagine it will feel pretty free when compared to prison. And, if it has a chance of benefiting you by helping you get released sooner, then it seems worth considering. There is a lot of heat in Morganton for someone trying to get through probation without a hitch. I want you to get out of prison, stay out, and live your best life. Hang in there. North Carolina started the initial phases of opening back up to the public, so maybe visitation will open up too.

Love,
Mom

Once I decided to sell the house, I started getting rid of things. Until that point, I had tried to preserve many of Ben's things for Simms and Rhett. But it was taxing to figure out what was most important and what should be sifted out. I was weary from spending so much time thinking about *things* and what to do with them. I had to lighten my load before the burden of it suffocated me.

In the purging process, I sold Ben's golf clubs, which sent Rhett reeling. They had been in the attic ever since the move, and he had never mentioned them, so I overlooked the importance of saving them. I was sad that my decision hurt Rhett, and I tried to get the golf clubs back—to no avail. But Rhett thought I had done it all with hurtful intention and reacted by lashing out on social media. He made slanderous remarks about my character and accused me of dishonoring his father. His verbal attack affected me deeply and inspired me to write this letter.

May 13, 2020
Dear Ben,

I love and miss you. I have honored your name to the best of my ability and will continue to do that for the rest of my life. I carry you with me and cherish all that you gave, all that we had.

I am letting go, as gracefully as I can, of material things, so that I can live the best life possible from here on for both of us. I imagine all the best for our sons, and I've tried my best to do right and good regarding them. I have no desire to hurt anyone, ever.

Sharing life with you taught me many things. One thing I learned is that I never have to let anyone treat me badly. If someone treats me badly, I walk away from it and try not to engage. This is what I have to do. You taught me that I have a right to be happy and live my own life. I have tried to help our sons learn the same thing because I want them to experience that freedom. It is my dream that all people experience the freedom of living life on their own terms.

To honor your memory, and to fulfill the request of your last will and testament, I went to Wrightsville Beach on March 8, 2016, with both our sons. There, we scattered your ashes in the waves. I miss you across the ocean and back so many times. Recently, I finally gave myself permission to be happy and free. I thought I had done it before, but it's a process, I guess.

I carry you with me always, and realize that I do not have to carry all your things around anymore. Of course, there are sentimental things that I want to keep. I also realize our sons would like to have some of your belongings. I've tried to consider and plan for this by holding on to some of your things as I wait for them to get a little more settled. But now, I am ready to spend my time living—not carrying unnecessary possessions around.

Ultimately, someone has to be an adult. Someone has to do the hard things. And I cannot live to please others. I will not ask permission for the way I live, and I will not enable those who use words and deeds for destructive purposes. I cannot give them my consideration or attention, even if I love them and care about them—even if they are family. I must go forward, into the light, engaging with others who are reasonable and respectful of things and people. I have tried to be generous and loving. Now, it is time to rise above destructive forces, allow others to live as they choose, and let go of those who cling to negative emotions like resentment, fear, greed, and envy. I will hold love and hope in my heart always—for you, our sons, and for humanity.

Love always,
Champ

CHAPTER 28

May 17, 2020

Dear Simms,

When you called yesterday, I was hiking in the woods, so I sat down on a big log covered in the kind of fungus that is crunchy and looks like little gray scales. As I scanned the forest for the words to say and listened to you, I found myself doing one of the hardest things I have ever done. I told you that I decided not to disclose my new home address to anyone. It felt like my heart was ripping in half, like what I imagine a mother feels when she hands her baby over for adoption.

I had always imagined having a home my sons could visit, but I need some control over my own life, and this is the only way I can figure out how to feel safe right now. I want to trust you—and I do trust your good intentions. However, I do not trust what might happen around you because of prison and your addiction. I need a safe place.

Okay, if I am honest with myself, I need to run away and hide for a while. I feel afraid sometimes—a lot lately. My soul has been tossed to weariness on the tumultuous sea of this ordeal. And I know yours has too. Being your mother is one of the biggest blessings of my life. I love you so much that my heart can hardly bear it. And I feel that way about Rhett too, even though he lashes out like a wounded animal whenever I try to show him love. It makes me cry when I think about how our plan for your release fell apart.

But, like so many other things in life, I know it is all happening for a reason. I believe that everything will fall into place as it should. Although I thought Morganton would be my home for a long time, perhaps it was just a waypoint, a place for me to learn about myself and find my bearings in the wake of your father's death.

Hopefully, I have a lot of life left. And I don't want to spend it managing property. I wanted you and Rhett to have a home, but maybe it is time for both of you to make your own homes. I wanted you to have a home when you got out of prison. But after they rejected your home plan and things started falling apart, I began to realize there are many ways I can show you love and support, even if I do not have a home for you.

I do not want you to feel like you have to take care of me or make things better between me and Rhett. In fact, I do not want you worrying about him, either. You have earned the right to be free and happy, just as I have. Do not let anyone take that away from you. You are a beautiful soul, and the world needs your light.

So, go out there and shine, knowing that you can message or call me anytime, and I'll be so happy to hear from you. I want to be available to spend time with you and continue the close relationship we have fostered during your incarceration. I hope you know that you will always be a priority in my life. I love you more than all the water in the ocean!

I am rooting for your happiness and freedom, so you can experience the wonder of life. I want you in my life for the rest of my life, to share in your joy as you find what is best for you. I just need to feel safe. And right now, it feels like that means having a home that's off the record—completely!

I believe we both desire freedom to live life fully without guilt or obligation. We want true relationships, love, romance, friendship, and a sense of belonging that transcends all fleeting circumstances. You belong in my heart always—and in my life, as much as you want to be in it. We have both invested a lot in our relationship. As a result, we have learned to be authentic with each other. I hope you will always feel free with me—free to say your truest thoughts, to share your deepest fears, and to exclaim your greatest dreams. I am grateful, beyond words, for our connection. It is strong enough to remain through any distance of space, time, or dimension. I look forward to having some adventures together when you get out of prison. And most of all, I look forward to following your journey through life as your biggest fan. I love you, son!

You are all grown up now. You have done your best to hold on to the goodness in your heart. You have looked inside yourself and found that life and peace are there, waiting for you to nurture them. Love is there. It shines over the world around you as you kindle the flames of self-reliance, recognizing the almighty power that abides in you. Trust yourself and know that all knowledge and power live inside you. Trust that power. Ask God for wisdom and know that you have it. I hope to see you soon.

Love,
Mom

~

June 5, 2020
Dear Simms,
When I spoke with you yesterday, my heart rejoiced to hear you making plans for your future. And guess what? Your original home plan for Morganton got approved! After I could not get the probation officer in Morganton to return my calls, I went up to

the office looking for him. He was gone for the day, but someone gave me his supervisor's name and number. After speaking with his supervisor, the PO finally called back the following week. We set up a time for him to meet me at the house for another review.

When I met him at the house, the parole officer was amiable and positive. After I told him the tenants should be out by June 20, he agreed to approve the plan. Additionally, he gave me the name and number of a contact at a drug treatment facility in Black Mountain where he believes you could get a job. So, we have a plan for your release! The rest we can figure out as we go along. I hope you feel as much relief as I do.

Love,

Mom

To my dismay, Rhett moved out on Saturday, June 20. When I delved into cleaning up and making repairs, the gun safe glared at me, reminding me that I could not have guns in the house if I planned on letting Simms live there. According to North Carolina General Statutes 14-415.1, it is "illegal for anyone who has been convicted of a felony to buy, own, possess, or have in their control any firearm or any weapon that could cause mass death or destruction." Considering the whole picture, I had three choices: find storage and care for guns I did not want, sell the guns for a good chunk of change (which I believed would be morally wrong because of their sentimental value to my sons), or give them to Rhett. Realizing the next day was Father's Day made the decision a little easier. Hoping I would not have to regret it later, I issued a pardon and gave the guns to Rhett.

By Monday afternoon, Smokefoot Trade and Loan harbored a banished gun safe, and my house bellowed with pride over a new AC unit. Furthermore, with the house vacant and the guns gone, I had accomplished the conditions of Simms's home plan. Soused in relief, I nourished my tattered house and sang sentimental songs of gratitude.

And as I reconnected with my home, I understood that my plans to sell the house were based on fear and desperation. With my thoughts clear and my concern over the eviction behind me, I soon realized I wanted to keep my home in Morganton.

I will not run away or hide. I will live and love—boldly, deeply, sweetly.

～

July 11, 2020

On July 2, I started to feel a little off. The next day was Friday, and I was tying up loose ends in Morganton so I could go back to Grant's place in the mountains. In my busyness, I ignored the mild ache in my head and did not think much of the tingly feeling in my throat, thinking my symptoms were from overwork and dusty deep cleaning.

When I arrived at Grant's house that night, I felt exhausted and hungry. I showered, ate a hearty meal, and settled down for a few minutes on the couch, trying to recover from a long, hard day. That's when I realized my symptoms might be associated with COVID-19. I shared my suspicions with Grant and quarantined myself in a separate part of the house that night. By morning, I had a low-grade fever and chills. My throat felt a little sore, and I had significant drainage in my sinuses. In an effort to keep Grant from being exposed, I headed back to Morganton for quarantine and made plans to get tested for COVID-19.

When I returned to Morganton, I did not know where to go for testing. The first place that popped up on my search was an urgent care office. After going there to inquire and learning that it would cost several hundred dollars to be tested there without insurance, I decided to wait until Monday and call the health department. Early Monday morning, I called and left a message, and when nobody answered, I drove to their office. I found a line of cars and saw people were being tested from their vehicles. About an hour and a half later, it was my turn.

The health care worker inserted a long swab up each nostril and held it there for several seconds. The procedure made my nose burn, and the swab was held very high in my nose. It felt similar to the sensation of getting water up my nose. When the test was complete, the nurse told me to stay quarantined until they called with results.

"You'll receive a call within three to five days," she mumbled in a monotone voice that matched the weariness in her eyes.

That Friday morning, they called with a positive test result and instructed me to remain in quarantine until ten days from onset of symptoms, or longer if symptoms persisted. The woman who gave me instructions over the phone said if I was symptom-free after ten days, my quarantine would be complete.

I am thankful that my case was only slightly more severe than a typical common cold—mostly because of the variety of symptoms and their determination to manifest on a surprising schedule. For example, after the fourth day, I thought I was going to recover quickly. Then, another wave of symptoms reared its head and tried to hold me down a bit longer. I suspected that my case was exacerbated by my circumstances with deep cleaning my house, which involved using respiratory irritants to combat the flea infestation. I was determined to resolve the problem using natural products, which meant I needed to use a lot of clove oil and other essential oils. With my sense of smell gone because of COVID-19, I was exposed to a lot of concentrated clove oil while I was sick without realizing how much of it I was inhaling. Perhaps I would have had a milder case without the extenuating circumstances. Either way, I am thankful that I made a complete recovery.

Yesterday, I finally got to speak with Simms on the phone after almost a month. We were both concerned about not being able to talk to each other, and Simms did not receive the letter I had sent with my new phone number. When he finally reached me, I updated him about some things regarding the house and told him that some of his things were missing. I had tried to save the things most important to Simms, but many of them were gone when I went to clean up the property after Rhett moved out. I hoped that Rhett was keeping them safe for Simms until his release.

Either way, Simms took it all in stride and remained focused on the important things—freedom and life in the present moment. Things are just things. Sometimes, they are sentimental, and the idea of losing them magnifies for a time. The things that matter most are in our hearts—the memories of love and times spent together.

I sat at the Grind Cafe, feeling the cool morning air. Birds sang around me as I typed outside and counted my blessings. Leaf shadows danced on the wooden table, and my coffee offered steamy comfort. Words of greeting from familiar faces kindled the flame of my simple life. They smiled and spoke my name with kindness. We exchanged pleasantries and asked about each other.

I savor the flavor of belonging and imagine a moment very soon when I will hug Simms again. He will walk out of that prison, and we will drive away together as he begins another chapter of his life.

CHAPTER 29

July 15, 2020

Dear Simms,

There are a lot of things I want to tell you now about being an adult. Many of them you have learned already. However, I am compelled to express them here as references, reminders, or simply reliefs from frustration. Additionally, I feel the need to cover my bases a little better this time with regard to tenancy.

I count on other people to learn things and know things, but when the outcomes of others' actions affect me, it is time for me to express myself regarding my own property and my own life. So, please know that what I write here is not assuming that you need me to tell or teach you any of these things. I am not even assuming that you need any instruction at all. I am simply providing information in order to be proactive regarding the care of my home and my own well-being.

I have been cleaning up the house since Rhett moved out. You no doubt remember that he wanted a cat and talked me into letting him have one by complaining that I had not explicitly stated "no pets" in the lease he signed. It makes me angry now that I gave in to yet another of his arguments. I allowed myself to be manipulated. But I have learned my lesson. Remember that I am expressing my frustration here, but it is not toward you. I just need to make sure some things that happened in that situation do not happen to me again.

I will start by saying that my house in Morganton is my home. When I stay with Grant, I feel at home because I love him and he makes me feel welcome. However, my home in Morganton is a priority. It is the place where I do things my way without infringing on the rights of anyone else. It is my domain —the place where I am queen.

During the past few weeks, I have been trying to get the house back in good repair, which required a lot of elbow grease. The downstairs level was infested with fleas! Some people would just use a poisonous flea bomb to take care of the problem. But I try to avoid harmful chemicals. And it is much more difficult to eradicate pests with natural methods once they get out of control. For this reason, I had to remove the large wool rug and have it professionally cleaned. Additionally, I have treated the house three times so far, using natural products with essential oils. And treatment must continue for several more weeks to ensure any remaining eggs, larvae, and pupae get eliminated. Therefore, no pets will be allowed on my property. And if I find out that any animal has been allowed in my house, that will be grounds for immediate eviction.

And while we are on the subject, I will go over my expectations regarding the care and maintenance of our home. First of all, I will have access to the entire home at all times. Let me reiterate that the house in Morganton is my refuge and my home. While you are living there, I would like to offer you two rooms, plus shared access to the other rooms on the lower level. The upstairs unit will be my private space. You may access it for emergencies, but there should be no need for you to use the upper level for daily living. This will help minimize cleaning and maintenance.

Downstairs, you will have a bedroom and another room

where you can keep all of your things. I am not interested in going into your private space. However, I will do so when necessary to ensure the space is clean and in good repair. Keep belongings out of the common areas and avoid cluttering your rooms. In the two rooms where you are allowed to keep your belongings, there are adequate drawers and closets for you to keep things organized, tidy, and clean. I also want you to keep the drawers in order. Keep all visible surfaces clean and uncluttered. Keep the lower level of the house vacuumed and dusted.

The kitchen should be cleaned completely after every use. Please report any maintenance issues promptly. Dishes are to be washed, dried, and put away immediately after use. All food items should be sealed and put away in closed cabinets or in the refrigerator. All kitchen and bathroom surfaces should be wiped after use. Keep the stovetop clean to avoid attracting pests. Use foil or a liner to prevent spillage in the oven.

Use a cleaning cloth with a bit of mild detergent to wash the bathtub and sink every few days to avoid buildup of grime. Rinse the tub and sink thoroughly after washing. Use a small amount of mild detergent on the toilet scrubber to clean the toilet bowl every few days. Use a cleaning cloth with lemon cleaner or detergent to wipe all the surfaces of the toilet. Wash the cleaning cloths regularly and keep them in the laundry room.

Dust furniture by dampening a cleaning cloth with hot water and squeezing it out very well. Then, wipe it over any dusty or soiled surfaces. A few drops of lemon essential oil can be added to the cloth if desired.

While you are living at home, I will not allow you to collect items for selling and trading. I need to have things simple and uncluttered. That is the way I want my property. If you need to collect things, you will have to find another location for storage. Nothing will be stored in the outbuildings or in the yard. Thank you for understanding the hardness of my tone in this letter as I try to clarify expectations so we can enjoy living together.

I am elated that you will be free soon. I love you, son.

Devotedly,

Mother

August 7, 2020

I went to Mountain View Correctional early Friday morning to await Simms's release. My heart thumped with joy and excitement as I walked from my car toward the front door with my phone. I wanted to take a video of him emerging from the darkness of incarceration into the light of freedom. As I approached the front of the prison, a guard came out and addressed me gruffly.

"Ma'am, you need to put your phone away," the short, pudgy man with a gun on his hip said.

"I'm here to pick up my son. He is supposed to be released today. I just want to document his release," I said.

"You can't use your phone here, ma'am. You need to go back to your car and wait," the man said in a serious tone that made me feel like a criminal.

My heart raced with anxiety as the coldness of the man's words tried to squash my joy with fear—fear that Simms might not get released because of my actions. I remembered all the other times I had come to the various prisons with a positive attitude and been reprimanded for one thing or another. Sometimes, I was standing in the wrong place for too long. Other times, I was walking to the wrong place at the wrong time, or turning around before I was told. It was as if they were determined to make me feel like a criminal for merely showing up at their institution to associate with an inmate.

But I reminded myself that they could not steal my joy today.

I watched from my car for about an hour before I saw Simms come through the cold metal door and walk toward my car. I got out but didn't dare walk toward him for fear that they would arrest us both for breaking some fucked up rule about being too happy.

When he got to the car, we put his bag of belongings in the trunk and drove away as quickly as we could—both worried that they might change their mind at any moment and make him stay.

"Whoa!" Simms said, grabbing for something to hold on to as I accelerated up the hill toward the main road.

Adjusting to riding in a car would be the first of many unexpected hurdles he would encounter on his journey of adaptation to the free world. Before his release, I had imagined taking him from prison to get some delicious food he had missed during his incarceration. But things would not be that simple. As I soon realized, each area of human development is affected by incarceration. Simms would face challenges in the physical, social, emotional, and cognitive domains.

Since the guards at the prison were determined to rain on our freedom parade, we saved our hugs and cheers until we got to Brown Mountain Overlook on the way down to Morganton from Spruce Pine, North Carolina. When we parked there, I asked someone to take our picture together. It was a cloudy day in the pictures, but in my imagination, the sky was brilliant blue and the sun shone in all its radiant glory.

CHAPTER 30

When Simms first returned home from prison, we both expected challenges. He wanted to find a doctor and get started on medication-assisted treatment right away. After he took care of that, he bought a used car with the money he had saved before going to jail. However, he did not go out much for the first few months. Based on our conversations, he was overwhelmed by the amount of activity involved in everyday life outside of prison. It was physically and mentally taxing. So, he rested a lot. Gradually, he built up his strength to deal with all the intricacies of typical daily activities. We talked about how things were going occasionally, but we were not visiting the way we had when he was in jail. I was trying to give him space to find his way as a man without a hovering mother.

After Christmas 2020, which we spent together, I started to notice changes in Simms. He was seeing a girl regularly, and I had overheard them arguing a couple of times. My mother's intuition told me that he was having trouble with his recovery. At that time, he was participating in a medical study to obtain his medication (Suboxone) in Wilmington. For this reason, he had to go to Wilmington once a month to get his medication and fulfill the obligations of the study.

During his February trip, Simms's car broke down on the way to Wilmington, and he called me for help. Simms likes to be independent and solve problems on his own, so when he called and asked me for the phone number for AAA, my intuition told me something was wrong. I looked up the number and texted it to Simms while concern quickened my heartbeat.

He can easily do a search to find the number for triple A, I reasoned. *So, he either just needs to talk to me for moral support through his crisis, or he is sinking emotionally from stress, relapse, or both.*

But I was several hundred miles away, which meant I would have to wait and see what transpired for a bit before taking any drastic action. Feeling empathetic about his car trouble and concerned about the stress he was under, I prayed for wisdom and tried to calm my weary heart, feeling like I could not take any more unfortunate complications.

Meanwhile, Simms messaged later and indicated he was figuring things out. He needed a mechanic, and it was too late in the day for that, so he would have to stay the night in Lumberton, where his car had stopped running. He pushed it to a gas station and received permission to leave it there overnight. We both searched for hotels and taxi services in the area, and I finally found reasonable accommodations. However, finding a ride to the hotel ended up being harder than one might imagine. None of the services were local.

After a lot of dead-end calls, Simms asked a guy who stopped at the gas station about getting a ride. Fortunately, the man was friendly and agreed to take Simms and his girlfriend to their hotel, which ended up being about a thirty-minute drive.

When Simms offered to pay for the ride, the good Samaritan said, "How about five dollars?"

It was after midnight by the time Simms arrived at the hotel and settled in for the night. I was relieved to know he was safe and hoped the remainder of the ordeal went a little easier on him.

The next day, Simms found out the motor in his car was ruined. But by then, he had built some problem-solving momentum. We talked on the phone a couple of times as he searched for a replacement vehicle and made plans to have his broken car towed back home.

Maybe I'm being paranoid by thinking he might have relapsed, I considered, determined not to worry as I waited for him to come back home. And even though I often felt emotionally spent, I knew I could not turn my back on Simms. Through it all, I believed he had loved and respected me as well as he could.

One moment at a time, I resolved. *I will remain in the eternal moment. I will love my son now. I will not give up on him, I told myself, trying to muster the will required to engage as my depleted soul resisted and cried to run away. If he gets arrested and goes back to jail, I just don't know how I am going to take another step.*

"God, please help us. Please, please help us," I cried aloud.

And before he left for his next trip to Wilmington, I looked him in the eyes and told him, "I don't know if I can be there for you if you go back to jail again. I have done all I can of that. I deserve to have some peace and joy. I need some relief."

Simms said he understood. But the conversation was clouded by his drooping eyes and nodding head. My heart sank to see him like that. I was devastated and afraid for him—and for myself.

He returned from that trip after about ten days looking like he had been put through an old-fashioned clothes wringer. My concern increased as he stayed away from home most nights and avoided me.

One morning, his parole officer stopped by, but Simms was not at the house. When I saw the white public safety car drive up outside, I was stricken with panic. At first, I thought I would not be able to go to the door. My heart pounded so hard and loud that

I felt sick—like I might faint. I took a deep breath and told myself to calm down. After several more breaths for each knock on the door, I filled my lungs with air and marched down the stairs to answer. I felt guilty about some unknown crime, and I was sure the officers would see it all over my face. My hands were shaking when I opened the door, and my eyes opened wide like a deer in headlights.

"Where is he?" the officer asked, standing close to the door in his bulletproof vest. We had developed a good rapport, so he skipped the cordiality.

"I don't know," I said. "I'll try to call him."

I dialed his number a couple of times, to no avail. Then, I sent him a text telling him to call. There was no reply.

He is somewhere in a deep opioid slumber at best, I thought.

"Has he been staying here?" the officer asked, staring hard at me as if I were the criminal.

I could feel the cortisol rushing through me, tearing my body apart. I was so tired. My eyes glossed over with tears, and my lips started to tremble, no longer able to handle the pressure he was putting on me about why Simms was not at home and where he might be.

"Sometimes," I said.

"Tell him to call me. I told him I have to see him every time he gets back from Wilmington," he said. "How's he doing?"

I shrugged my shoulders, trying to hide the terror running through my body. *How could he get into this situation again?* I wondered. *I can't do this anymore.*

"Do you think he's relapsed?" he continued.

I stared at him in silence, not wanting to betray my son, wondering how to get out of the predicament.

"Does he have a girlfriend?" the officer asked.

"Yes, but I told her she can't be here anymore. Then, he started staying out, so I guess he is staying with her sometimes," I explained.

"Who is she?" he asked.

I told the officer her name and gave him a general idea of where she lived. I knew this because when I suspected he had relapsed, I came home from Grant's house in the mountains and went downstairs to take action. I told her we needed to talk and asked her to come upstairs. Like me, she didn't want to betray Simms, but she wanted to help him and knew he needed to change something. In response to my interrogation, she shared some personal information about herself. Her concerns about Simms's drug abuse were obvious during our conversation. So, I took further action.

"Get your things. I'm taking you home. You can't come here anymore. It's not personal, but I have to help my son. Right now, it doesn't seem good for you to be here," I told her.

When we arrived at her house, I made it clear that she was not to be on my property for any reason. I needed to do everything possible to get things under control before Simms ended up back in prison.

When I returned home, I told Simms we had to have a meeting. He was in no shape for it at the time, so I waited, knowing he had to be ready to talk in order for us to have an effective conversation about getting him back on track. After harping on him via text for a few days, we finally found ourselves in the same room, ready for a serious conversation.

March 3, 2021

Simms sat down on our red couch, and I sat in a corner chair, not knowing what I would do or say. My plan was to listen and wait for wisdom before speaking or acting. I got up from my chair and sat down beside him on the couch. Then, I took his hand and held it for a minute in silence before turning his palm up and noticing the red track marks.

In the days prior, when I began to suspect a relapse, I had heard him in the bathroom crying out in pain. It was unlike him, so I asked what was wrong. He snapped at me and said he was constipated. But my instinct told me it was something worse.

"Can you tell me about this?" I asked calmly as I pointed to the three red marks on the inside of his forearm.

He looked at me with steady eyes and remained silent. I stared back into his deep blue eyes as I searched for wisdom.

"When did it start?" I asked. "What triggered it?" I paused. "And how can I help?"

"You're doing it," he said. "Just love me and let me handle it. I'm working on getting back on track. But it takes time."

"But I'm concerned for you, Simms. You're at risk of going back to jail. And if that happens, I don't know if I can be the person who helps you through that again. I'm weary. I want to live my life with some joy and peace," I told him as I stared earnestly into his eyes. "I just wonder if I need to make you do something. Do I need to make the choice and force you to go to detox or something? Because I know that when you need more heroin, the craving is so powerful that it causes you to take risks you cannot afford to take. Also, there is the danger of overdose and death, which really freaks me out. I love you so much, Simms. And it's upsetting to see you struggling with this. I don't want to lose you."

"Mom, what you're doing now is the only way you can help me—by loving me, talking to me, and trying to understand, by being patient with me as I try to get myself back on the Suboxone full-time." He paused, and I waited. "This is my battle, Mom. And I have to fight it myself. Sure, there's a chance I might lose it. But if I don't fight it myself, I can't win it, either. Believe me, I want to win it, and I think I can. But even if I don't, it will never be your fault. There is nothing else you can do aside from what you've done—and what you're doing now by having this conversation with me. You mean the world to me,

Mom. And I can't thank you enough for all you've done to help me. Thank you for not giving up on me. I really want to win this fight. Nobody else can win it for me. I have to do it myself. I can do this, Mom. Please don't worry."

Simms and I continued to dissect the events that led to his relapse in an effort to avoid future problems. As we talked, I learned more about the nature of opioid addiction, the availability of various types of opioids, and their unique effects.

As Simms explained his personal battle with opioid addiction, I learned more about the process of withdrawal. Because of PAWS, detoxing from opioids does not help an addict stop abusing the drug. The addict must desire recovery and take necessary steps to change their habits.

Unfortunately, when an addict uses an analog, things become very dangerous and serious. Because the addictive nature of these chemicals is extremely powerful, Simms was facing a complex problem on his journey to recover from relapse. He explained his plan to me in a way that helped me understand the dynamics of transitioning from a powerful analog opioid to medication-assisted treatment for opioid dependence. I would have to be patient and hope that he would recover.

"I just want you to be safe and keep trying," I said. "As long as you keep trying, I'm going to keep trying because I love and trust you, even though it's hard, even though I get tired and apprehensive."

"I love you too, Mom."

"I can't stop trying if you don't stop trying. Now, keep your butt here, at home, five nights a week!" I said firmly, pointing my finger downward for emphasis. "And I mean it!"

"I will," Simms said, nodding his head and gazing hard into my eyes to tell me he was serious.

～

Even though I wanted to keep supporting Simms's recovery, I did not want to overlook my own right to have peace in my life. I told him I wanted to video chat with him every day for a while. This is because I was still staying at Grant's place a lot. I wanted to know how he was doing each day so I could monitor his progress and stay home more if necessary.

In addition to talking about his addiction and the process of recovering from relapse, we discussed my expectations related to housekeeping, visitors, and community involvement. When I suggested employment, he told me he already had a job—one that was enjoyable and rewarding to him. He told me he takes pride in what he does as a networking agent. He is naturally good at connecting with people, remembering details, and recognizing ways to maximize business potential through relationships. I understood his desire to work for himself, as his father had been mostly self-employed too. For this reason, I told him I supported his decision to work for himself.

"But I still think it would be beneficial for you to have a regular responsibility within the community," I said. "You either need to get a part-time job or volunteer at a local organization. I want you to have someone depending on you to show up somewhere on a regular basis. This is not negotiable. And I want to meet with you at least once a week for a while. Once a week in the evening, I'm going to come here and sit down with you. And we're going to talk." I paused for a minute, trying to make sure I made my expectations clear. I wanted him to know that I expected to see him working on his recovery every day. "Choose a day. Then, if something happens, we can change it. But you have to talk to me on video chat to change it. It's an official appointment."

"Uh, Wednesday is probably good," he said.

"Okay, so Wednesdays. What time?" I said.

"Seven o'clock?" he asked.

"Seven o'clock on the red couch, all right?" I said.

We both stood up and wrapped our arms around each other. I held him tightly and rubbed my hand over his back. *His shoulders and back are so much like his father's now that he's all grown up,* I thought.

"Thank you for your time, Simms. Have a good night."

"Thanks for yours, Mom," Simms said with a nod and a purse of his lips that was almost a smile. His eyes were clear, and I could tell he was sincere about his efforts toward recovery.

"I love you," I said one more time before ascending to my upstairs suite.

"Love you too, Mom."

After our conversation about his relapse, Simms and I kept in closer touch when I was out of town and had our regular couch meetings, as we had planned. Additionally, Simms found a job delivering pizza a few nights a week. I continued encouraging healthy foods, outdoor time, and exercise through modeling and directly suggesting specific food items such as kale, berries, legumes, and oatmeal. I prompted him to go outside when the weather was nice and advised him to take walks. Simms respectfully acknowledged my input and occasionally integrated my suggestions into his routine.

Changing the habits he had developed in prison was proving to be a much longer process than I expected, but I tried to be patient. As the months passed from March to June, Simms stabilized in his recovery and developed regular routines with his job and his girlfriend. We had conversations about self-care and maintenance of living spaces, including instruction on how to clean a bathroom and keep desks and counters clutter-free.

In August, I started to wonder how to help Simms live on his own. Having always wanted independence for my sons, I was torn between my protective instincts as his mother and my own

PART IV

AFTERWORD

Ever since we decided to collaborate on writing this memoir, Simms and I have agreed on the main purpose of our project—to make our tragic experiences count by sharing our story.

For this reason, when I asked Simms if I could interview him for our book, he said yes and wholeheartedly participated in the process.

Along with the following transcribed interview, Simms and I have included several other sections here that may lead to additional understanding and prompt productive discussions about topics related to our story.

TRANSCRIBED INTERVIEW

INTERVIEWER: CINNAMIN INTERVIEWEE: SIMMS

August 12, 2021

Cinnamin: When did you first use opioids?

Simms: The first time I tangled with opioids, I was sixteen and dating a girl named Kelly. Her mother had knee replacement surgery and came home with a generous supply of opioids— most of which made their way to me. That led to a period of prolonged use that resulted in significant discomfort when it ended.

Cinnamin: Do you believe that someone could have helped you realize the consequences of opioid use and addiction before you started using? If so, how?

Simms: I'm not sure if any words could have helped me understand the consequences of opioid use and addiction. I just wanted to learn everything firsthand, for myself. I believe it's something you can only realize once you're neck deep into it. An addict experiences subtle, psychological changes over time that add up. But those changes cannot be effectively described with words.

Cinnamin: What can parents do to protect their children from drug addiction?

Simms: The most important thing a parent can do to

discourage drug experimentation in their children is to be honest about their own experiences, or lack of experience, with drugs. If you're a parent and you have limited or no personal experience with drugs, share what you know about other people who have been negatively affected by drug abuse. Even if you feel uncomfortable about it or do not know exactly what to say, just open up to your kids and have honest conversations about what you know, what happened to you, and what happened to others. Be specific so that they can get as accurate an idea as possible about the consequences related to drug use.

Cinnamin: What role did opioid addiction play in your legal troubles?

Simms: I believe that my addiction is responsible for my arrest and all my legal troubles. I was arrested for selling and distributing drugs. And I think I got into that because I was looking for a way to fund my addiction. A lot of people get money for drugs by stealing from their family members, friends, or coworkers. Others commit robbery or fraud to fund their drug habits. In my case, I didn't want to commit crimes against innocent people like that. I wanted to fund my drug use in a way that would be easier on my conscience. When a person buys drugs, they consent to the deal. So, selling drugs to earn money for my own drug use seemed like the most honest way to do it.

Cinnamin: How do you stay motivated in your recovery?

Simms: I would say it's pretty easy for me to stay motivated in my recovery because it's easy for me to see all the progress I'm making. And I can feel it accumulating all the time. Even if other people can't see the progress I'm making, I know how much progress I'm making, and I know where I stood before and where I stand now. I continue to see how far I've come, and I'm just proud of myself for it.

Cinnamin: So, what about financial issues related to medication-assisted treatment?

Simms: Well, that's a big problem right now, especially with buprenorphine because the treatment is so popular and helpful. And it's in such high demand that a lot of doctors and practitioners and other people in the recovery community are getting into the business and taking advantage of the need there is for it.

For instance, a good way to measure this is to look at the black market for buprenorphine. There's a huge demand for the drug on the street, even though it's very easy to get and readily available. I mean, honestly, all that's required for a person to get a prescription is for them to walk into one of these offices with enough money and say, "I have cravings to use opiates." You don't even have to be actively using opiates to get the medication. If you just say, "I have a history of use and I'm worried I'm going to start using again, so I want to get on these," then they'll put you right on, but there's no other requirement to get a prescription besides wanting to have them.

Yet there's still a huge black market for it because there's not enough people available to prescribe it, and it costs too much to get it prescribed. Almost all of it that is bought on the street is used by people not trying to get high but people who are actually trying to better their lives. A lot of people start buying them on the street because they can't afford to keep getting high and keep buying heroin, or pills, or whatever. And so, they start buying subs. And a lot of people, after they start subs, they don't go back to getting high because it's a lot cheaper. It lasts longer, and it's just a huge weight off their shoulders to be able to get off that hamster wheel and feel like a normal person again. Then, the longer they use them, the more they can see and feel their life coming back together.

So, the black-market demand for it just shows how much of a need there is for this opiate treatment. But it can cost as much as a thousand dollars a month, just to get a prescription for buprenorphine. That's four to six hundred dollars for the doctor's visit, which often isn't covered by insurance, and then a few hundred dollars for the medication at the pharmacy, if you don't have insurance to cover it. Thankfully, there are a lot of programs out there to help people get the medication. Methadone clinics now offer buprenorphine, as well. And a lot of them will even allow you to keep coming and getting your medication for free if you can't afford to pay. So, there are ways around. But in general, the treatment is very expensive, and often, if you call around and check all the offices where they are offering buprenorphine treatment, they'll often have long waiting lists.

You might have to wait a month or two before you're even able to get an appointment and get in there. And these opioid users on the street who've pulled together enough money for a doctor's appointment to get medication-assisted treatment with buprenorphine don't have two months to wait. They probably won't have the money in 48 hours. They need to be able to go in and get that treatment now, and it's a miracle if they even get the money together and want to use it for that instead of another high.

Cinnamin: Tell me about the strong analog opioids and how they complicate recovery.

Simms: Well, especially with fentanyl, there are so many analogs, which are drugs that share the chemical structure and characteristics of a drug with slight alterations that change the effects somewhat by making it more potent or more long lasting. Or sometimes it's altered for no other reason than to work around controlled substance laws. They make a new drug that has not been made illegal yet. They can't grow enough heroin to support the American demand for opioids. So, they have to rely on extremely strong opioid analogs that are made in labs.

So, these fentanyl analogs are very lipid soluble and build up in fatty tissue, and they make it harder to transition on to buprenorphine because it takes a much longer time for it to get out of your system, even though the fentanyl high might only last a couple of hours. Then, a few hours after a dose, an opiate user will be sick and need to use something again. It can take as few as four days and as many as twenty-six days for a synthetic opioid analog to clear a person's system, depending on frequency of use, amount of adipose tissue, and other factors. And until it's all completely worked out of the system, a person cannot be successfully induced onto buprenorphine. So, a heroin addict might go out on the street to get heroin and get something a hundred times more powerful—definitely more than he or she bargained for.

REFLECTIONS ON INCARCERATION

By Simms

The psychological effects of incarceration are broad, powerful, and overwhelmingly negative. People who have never been locked up are sometimes under the impression that doing time is easy, possibly even viewing it as a break from life and responsibilities. I can attest, from personal experience, that it is anything but. It may seem easy since it's not a physically demanding task. Someone locked up doesn't pay bills, go to work (sometimes), support others, do chores, or do many other tasks that free people might see as burdensome.

However, it is not that prisoners don't have to do these tasks, but rather that they do not get to do them. Although they may seem a burden to someone free, anyone incarcerated knows that to have options is a great privilege, as being locked up results in a lack of options. In most cases, incarceration does not take away responsibility. Instead, it prevents one from being able to fulfill obligations. Prisoners find themselves unable to support their families. Furthermore, a prisoner may need to depend on his family for support, both emotionally and monetarily.

Prison makes you feel like you can't go any lower and have

no ability to change things. You feel like you can't pick yourself up until you have waited out your time. Even the best days in prison feel like the worst days of your life. Prison seems to take away your humanity. You are denied most of the simplest pleasures in life. You are treated like less than a human in every way, from the food you eat to the medical treatment you receive —especially psychiatric treatment.

In prison, psychiatric care is reduced to three basic questions. Do you want to hurt yourself? Do you want to hurt others? And do you want to escape? These questions are designed to absolve the prison system of liability for anything and everything you do. Treatment for any of these symptoms consists of placing you on suicide watch, where you are stripped buck naked and put in solitary confinement with nothing but a foam mattress with no sheets or blanket or reading material until a psychiatrist deems that these symptoms are gone.

Prisoners decide that they are "happy" quickly after the minimum five to seven days on suicide watch, as they are quite miserable and ready to wear clothes again. Basically, they treat major depression by showing you how they can make your life worse! Many mainstream and first-line (the most effective) treatments for psychiatric disorders are not used in prisons for a variety of reasons. One reason is that people seek prescriptions for these drugs after they've had them prescribed in the free world. What the prison officials fail to realize is that people seek these medications because they are effective at relieving their symptoms. Instead of using mainstream, well-understood medications, the prisons often opt to use new experimental alternatives as blanket applications for almost all psychiatric conditions. I strongly suspect that they are rewarded financially, or otherwise, for this medical "research."

Prison is an extremely stressful environment. First of all, the population density within correctional facilities is extremely high; it's possibly one of the densest environments in the world. I currently reside in a room that I share with one other person. The size of this room is about the size of a king-sized mattress. This room is one of many in a three-story cell block that serves as a home for over one hundred people. The whole prison is about the size of a football field and houses one thousand people. It must also be taken into consideration that these are not one thousand average people. This is a thousand people who, for the most part, have proven to be the most intolerable, violent, thieving people society has to offer.

To be able to live with these people, you are forced to digress. There is no taking the high road. You must know how to be a thief in order to protect yourself from theft. You must become violent to save yourself from violence. People join gangs and extort people to protect themselves from other gangs and extortion. If you live here long enough, you will have to stoop down to their level just to get by.

You can try to be a model inmate, follow rules, keep to yourself, or rise above the crowd. But the guards will always see you as a bad guy at the end of the day. You are treated like a rule breaker because you are an inmate. The guards and staff feel justified in treating you poorly. This goes for guards, doctors, chaplains, nurses, and so on. The guards constantly blur the lines of the rules to exert more power over you whenever they want.

For instance, policy says you may only have twenty-five pictures at a time. I received sixty pictures in the mail at once. Now, no one ever enforces this rule. In general, many inmates have more than twenty-five pictures with their personal possessions. The sergeant, or the head guard, called me to his office to discuss the pictures that had been mailed to me.

The guard said, "You are only supposed to have twenty-five, but we both know how that goes. So, I will assume you have none already. Pick the ones you want to keep, and rest assured, I won't be counting them."

He proceeded to let me take all but a few pictures (more than twenty-five). Later, a guard did not like that I was promoted to medium custody, so he searched my room for a reason to write me up. He filed disciplinary action against me because I had too many pictures. Even if I had kept only twenty-five, they could decide to count magazine pages and drawings as pictures to push me over the limit. The point is that the guards want you to know that they can do whatever they want if they feel like it. This is in line with the famous Stanford prison experiment, where people put in the prison guard's role became sadistic in controlling and punishing people in the prisoner's role.

Going to prison is like dying in a lot of ways. For instance, when you die, everyone gives all your stuff away and forgets about you. When you go to prison, people give all your stuff away and forget about you. Preparing to go to prison felt like having a terminal illness and knowing I was about to die any day. It changed my behavior accordingly. I tried to make and save as much money as I could to help my family. Once I was no longer able to help them and became a financial burden, I relapsed to drug use a few times as I tried to cope with my impending incarceration. I felt as if all the positive progress I had made, and all my clean time, had not done anything to keep me from having to go to prison.

When you go to prison, it seems as if everything you have worked for and the life you have made are all lost, as if there is no way for you to maintain your assets. You can't pay rent for your house where your belongings and valuables are stored. You lose houses and cars because you can't make the payments. You can no longer work to support your family and loved ones, as working in prison only pays a dollar per day—not enough to live comfortably in prison, let alone help your children and family. Going to prison means you lose your job, no matter how good it is, how prestigious it is, or how long you have been there. Your relationships with most people will altogether cease to exist.

REFLECTIONS ON RECOVERY, MEDICATION-ASSISTED TREATMENT, AND RELATED DRUGS

By Simms

Closure can occur only with the formation of negative memories. Memories of withdrawal are not enough, as the relief of withdrawal by drug use outweighs the negative effects of withdrawal. The first time I went to jail, I was physically addicted to heroin. I was arrested for possessing and selling drugs illegally. Even though the charges against me were all drug related, I did not blame drugs for my incarceration. Instead, I rationalized how I wasn't hurting anyone, how I was doing fine —financially supporting myself by selling drugs, which I did not believe was wrong. I believed, and still believe, that people should have the right to make their own choices about drug use.

It is my opinion, based on my experience and observations, that criminalization of drug use exacerbates the negative impact. When nonviolent drug offenders end up with life-changing criminal records, the repercussions are devastating and irreversible. The loss of opportunities puts money in the hands of criminals, makes drugs more unsafe from a lack of quality control or regulation, and perpetuates criminal activity.

For example, a nonviolent drug dealer ends up in prison with other criminals. The dealer or addict is removed from potential recovery-program participation. Additionally, the stigma of incarceration adds to the complication of making a legal living after prison. In my opinion, making drugs illegal restricts access to more moderate, less harmful alternative drugs.

The bottom line is that I did not believe I had done anything wrong from the standpoint of my own personal value system. Therefore, I found myself ill-equipped to accomplish the process of closure in my relationship with addiction to opioids. Because I did not blame heroin for my incarceration, I missed using and felt angry at the forces that had torn us apart. My cravings were fueled by this intense anger, and the object of my rage was the legal system and its archaic, ineffective practices related to drug regulation policies and procedures.

After completely detoxing from heroin, I continued to crave it more than ever. I thought about it all day, talked about it, dreamed about it. No amount of time away from it in jail was ever going to make me get over it. I longed for the day when I could do it again. Not long after my release from jail, I resumed heroin use—my toxic relationship with no closure. I blew through what little money I had tucked away before going to jail. I had scored a construction job and spent all the money I made every day supporting my habit.

I was too overwhelmed with alleviating withdrawal symptoms to analyze the negative impact of heroin on my life. I spiraled to a low point where I was always broke and almost constantly dope sick. This was the first time I had to steal to support my addiction. One day, as I was going through withdrawals, I remembered what a very good friend who had gotten over heroin once told me.

He said, "The worst thing I ever did was sell my grandparents' silverware for heroin. I will never forget—not the anger but the pure disappointment when they found out."

Ultimately, my addicted brain took the information it needed and discarded the devastating reality of it. I stepped onto the slippery slope and began to take my own family's silver, squashing the gravity of my deed to the depths of my dope-sick soul. My family is the most important thing in the world to me. That silverware represented my family to me. When I sold it, I felt like I had chosen heroin over my family. I was disgusted with myself.

Reflecting on this event makes me even more grateful that treatment with Suboxone provided a way for me to break the vicious cycle. When I found stability in my treatment with Suboxone, I finally did not have to worry about how to ward off sickness every day. Instead, I was able to make long-term goals and plans for my life—to think about the things "normal" people think about. I could dream about a future and pursue intellectual and social interests.

Not too long after getting out of jail and getting out of control with heroin, I was ordered to participate in a recovery program as part of my probation. I began treatment with Suboxone and immediately started to feel hope that a future without heroin could be possible. I took the positive effects of Suboxone and used them to learn about myself. I started saving Suboxone, limiting myself as I gained more self-control and understanding of how the medication worked. Eventually, I had saved enough to last me a year, if needed.

In the drug community, people regularly call each other for help to score drugs. After I got off heroin and on Suboxone, I told people I couldn't find heroin when they asked because I didn't want anything to do with it. Additionally, I didn't want anything to do with the people who were using heroin—understanding their propensity to steal. All that matters to a heroin addict is one more fix to alleviate the sickness.

Heroin addicts often become depressed and nihilistic. My experience was no exception. The things I once enjoyed no longer brought me pleasure. Once a person experiences the unmatched euphoria of a heroin high, all other pleasure is distorted to a whole new low. Sports, exercise, food, sex, hobbies, and other interests fall by the wayside.

After a period of stability through treatment with Suboxone, I noticed that my mood and motivation had drastically improved. Once again, I began to feel joy in eating, sex, social interaction, exercise, video games, and outdoor activities. I started to put on healthy weight.

I have always found satisfaction in saving money. In fact, the only thing that has ever made me waste money without caring is heroin. After finding stability on Suboxone, I was able to start saving money again. With diligence, I got to a point where I could support myself financially. As I progressed in treatment, I began to reflect on the positive changes in my life associated with Suboxone treatment. My reflections provided a contrast, allowing me to see clearly how heroin had negatively impacted my life. This realization set in motion the process of ending my toxic relationship with heroin addiction.

My deep depression, which was a symptom of opioid abuse, diminished each day as I continued using Suboxone. The first Suboxone lasted me six days. Spending only fifteen dollars for a six-day supply was my first positive reinforcement. Before I started using Suboxone, I was spending fifty dollars a day, still felt sick, and didn't sleep well. Seeing clearly that I may have found my ticket back to life, I stopped buying heroin and bought only Suboxone. I was finally able to start saving money again, which was a huge relief.

To my despair, my drug dealer quickly decided he didn't want to sell me any more Suboxone since I was spending fifteen to thirty dollars per week instead of the previous two to three hundred dollars. I started looking for a new source for Suboxone. I used heroin again briefly during my search and fortunately found someone else willing to sell me Suboxone. I entered a period of stability for the first time since I had become addicted to heroin.

In my experience, the importance of Suboxone cannot be overstated. I once read an article by the World Health Organization about Suboxone. It explained how diverted, illegally sold Suboxone was not a problem, as all diverted Suboxone served its intended purpose of getting and keeping people off opioids. This is done because the only requirement to get a prescription for Suboxone is to have a desire or craving to use opioids. This means that, essentially, if I have a desire to use Suboxone, then I qualify for a prescription. Yet it is still controlled in a way that limits its access to people who need it because it is an expensive treatment. Additionally, the waiting list to see a doctor certified to prescribe it can be months long due to high demand. This leads to a time of waiting that an opioid addict cannot afford, resulting in relapse of heroin use.

Suboxone is gradually becoming more accessible. I believe it will soon become inexpensive and easy to obtain, as it takes center stage as our most powerful tool for fighting opioid addiction. You may wonder why it should be so easy to obtain, since it is an opioid capable of producing intoxication and euphoria. These qualities are certainly cause for alarm. However, Suboxone is different from traditionally abused opioids and other maintenance opioids, like methadone and LAAM (levacetylmethadol), in a few important ways. I believe these differences will be significant aspects of an effective model used in the creation of less abusable substitutes for other traditional drugs of abuse. Furthermore, these developments have the potential to help us better understand addiction altogether.

First of all, anyone can take Suboxone and become intoxicated, but only opioid addicts can tolerate the effects enough for it to be reinforcing. If someone who isn't already an opioid addict takes Suboxone, it will precipitate intolerable nausea and vomiting, as anyone who has experienced it can tell you. People not addicted to opioids who take Suboxone do not enjoy it. They become uncomfortably sick for hours and typically have no desire to take it again or repeat the experience. This alone is an amazing quality that sets Suboxone apart from other opioids of abuse.

Second, Suboxone can be used but arguably not abused in the usual sense of how drugs are abused. When we think of alcohol or other drugs that are typically abused, it is common sense that more drugs equals more intoxication. Not so with Suboxone. It has a ceiling effect. After a certain point, taking more does not produce any further effects. This is a phenomenon not seen in any other drugs of abuse, mostly because it makes a drug hard to abuse. The ceiling effect adds a layer of protection, making it extremely safe in the treatment of opioid addicts. However, even small doses will make an opioid-naïve person uncomfortably sick. Even still, large doses do not become increasingly dangerous. Suboxone does not have the deadly dose-dependent respiratory depression indicative of all other opioids. In fact, I have not been able to find a recorded case where Suboxone, taken in isolation, in any dose, has led to death.

Suboxone is reinforcing enough to make opioid addicts want to take it, but taking larger doses does not intensify the high experienced by the user. On top of this, since Suboxone has a maximum level of effect, if you take more without waiting until some leaves your system, it is not reinforcing. Furthermore, the effects become more reinforcing the longer a user waits between doses. Over time, this helps the opioid addict by allowing the brain to rewire its reward circuits, thereby providing the scaffolding needed for an addict to develop new behavioral patterns and self-discipline. The addict is rewarded for using consistent moderation. This may be the most important and amazing quality ever found in a drug. And it contrasts to hard drugs like heroin that encourage and reward overconsumption, impatience, and lack of self-control.

I began taking Suboxone several years ago. Over time, I have gradually reduced my dosage and increased the time between doses. The lower my doses, and the longer the time between doses, the more rewarding it becomes.

Additionally, Suboxone acts as an opioid antagonist. When someone takes Suboxone, the person is unable to get high from opioids while the treatment drug is active in their system. If heroin, or another opioid-based drug, is taken while Suboxone is active in the system, the person is incapable of getting high from the opioid use. This quality makes Suboxone impressively effective as a treatment tool, especially when used in conjunction with a holistic treatment program. When used properly under qualified supervision, Suboxone has enormous potential to save the lives of people who otherwise find themselves completely enslaved by their opioid addiction. In turn, families are spared the needless loss of loved ones, and addicts find hope to rebuild shattered dreams.

Suboxone is an effective treatment for opioid addiction because it addresses the intense cravings experienced by opioid addicts and empowers them to manage their life with fewer addiction-related complications.

Suboxone (buprenorphine and naloxone) and Subutex (buprenorphine) are brand names for buprenorphine products. These drugs are used in conjunction with other therapeutic practices to treat opioid addiction. Buprenorphine partially activates neurological opioid receptors throughout the body. Methadone, on the other hand, completely activates opioid receptors. All the drugs mentioned here are opioid agonists because they activate specific opioid receptors in the brain and body. But they have different efficacy levels. Full agonists are said to have 100% efficacy because they completely activate the receptor.

On the other hand, there are antagonists—drugs that attach to opioid receptors—which prevent opioids from attaching to the opioid receptors. Opioid antagonists can reverse overdose. Naloxone is one drug used for this purpose. It can be injected into muscle tissue or used as a nasal spray. Some addicts keep naloxone (brand name Narcan) on hand in case of emergencies. Naloxone can trigger withdrawal and intense pain as it blocks the effects of opioids. For this reason, addicts do not desire to use it or abuse it. Naloxone (Narcan nasal spray) can be purchased at pharmacies without a prescription.

If addicts are actively using a full agonist like heroin or methadone, they will experience withdrawal symptoms following treatment with naloxone or other opioid antagonists. Additionally, they will experience withdrawal and pain if they use a partial agonist like buprenorphine because its efficacy is only about 30%. For this reason, transition from active use of full agonist opioids to medication-assisted treatment with a partial agonist opioid like buprenorphine can be a challenging and complex process.

The process of transitioning to medication-assisted treatment is called induction. And as I mentioned, it can be complex, depending on the level of opioid abuse. A person who is struggling with high levels of opioid abuse may not be able to walk into a clinic and immediately take buprenorphine without entering serious withdrawal, which causes severe pain. Instead, they will have to work their opioid dosage down over several days until they get to the right level of withdrawal to be able to take buprenorphine without getting sick. This is where methadone can play an important role in the process of induction to medication-assisted therapy. It can help a person stop using illegal drugs while they transition.

There are several drawbacks to using methadone as a long-term treatment for opioid addiction. It can cause significant weight gain and interfere with the endocrine system. Additionally, it is usually given out in daily doses through certified clinics. Methadone treatment is a more intensive care program that tends to interfere more with daily life, since the patient has to integrate daily visits to a treatment clinic.

In contrast, buprenorphine can be dispensed in monthly prescriptions. The patient can take the medication independently each day without going to a clinic. This allows recovering addicts to travel and experience less interruption of daily life activities while still participating in a recovery plan.

Based on my personal experience with heroin addiction and medication-assisted treatment with Suboxone, I suggest that anyone struggling to overcome the devastation of opioid addiction consult their physician about Suboxone or other buprenorphine medications. There are many factors that contribute to a successful recovery, so it's important to work with a doctor who is experienced in heroin addiction recovery. Having a treatment plan that includes connection to a community and other behavioral approaches can greatly improve an addict's chances for successful recovery. A drug can only help a person when that person is ready and willing to participate in the holistic process of addiction recovery. Among the many negative effects of addiction is the burden of time wasted finding drugs, waiting on dealers, searching for new sources, and so on. Educational classes, work, hobbies, and time with friends or loved ones become sacrifices for the sake of satisfying an addict's cravings for opioids. The addiction overwhelms the addict and becomes a debilitating obsession. Suboxone can help the opioid addict return to a normal schedule.

When I finally got on a regular treatment schedule with Suboxone, it felt like a huge weight was lifted from my shoulders as I was able to stop worrying about where my next fix would come from. I felt like I had my life back with all the time not spent waiting on drug dealers. Although doctors can also seem slow at times, the routine is different and more conventional. So, I found myself able to break away from the drug lifestyle and begin to experience a lifestyle that felt more normal, healthier, more fulfilled, and free. The chains of addiction bound me so tightly at times that I felt I couldn't move, see, or feel. I was lost in a tumultuous ocean of shame and guilt. I couldn't seem to get to the shore until I found Suboxone. I am grateful that it helped me and want to encourage anyone who has not found a way out to consider consulting a health care professional about Suboxone treatment.

As I remained faithful to my rehabilitation, I found myself replacing old drug routines with new habits of working regularly, spending time with other friends who were not involved in illegal drug activities, hiking, and appreciating the everyday simple things in life, like the beauty of nature and the satisfaction found in conversation and shared activities. I felt myself emerging from the bondage of having to associate with other drug addicts. It was a relief because when addicts are abusing drugs, they cannot be trusted. The craving dominates their activities, decisions, and state of mind.

Treatment with Suboxone has led to a richer life experience for me. I am able to look at my previous activities from a distance and realize how tedious, destructive, inconvenient, and harmful my behaviors were before. After a while, I began to feel thankful for my new routines. I did not miss the stress and anxiety associated with my old drug lifestyle. I felt complete relief!

In addition to its effectiveness in alleviating the symptoms of opioid dependency and managing the symptoms of addiction, Suboxone is helpful from a psychological viewpoint. Often, illegal drug use can be linked to attempts at self-medication. Opioids are extremely addictive because using them temporarily alleviates symptoms of many psychological disorders: anxiety, paranoia, schizophrenia, and other mood disorders. However, the rebound effect, as the high from the drug wears off, magnifies the symptoms and triggers strong cravings for more relief. The cycle of addiction begins, and a person loses sight of everything that really matters. As the cycle continues, higher doses of the drugs are needed to produce the same effect, or the same level of relief from psychological symptoms. The increased dosage of drugs increases the intensity of the rebound effect, and a destructive spiral gains momentum, pulling the subject downward into an ever-deepening ravine of despair.

I have a history of various psychiatric disorders, including depression, bipolar disorder, ADHD, anxiety, conduct disorder, and oppositional defiant disorder. As a result of my symptoms and related behavior, I was admitted to a psychiatric institution in my youth, where I was treated with various psychiatric medications. I have taken a variety of prescribed medications over the years as my family tried to help me integrate and function in mainstream society. Additionally, I have experimented with and used drugs illegally to self-medicate. Some medications helped, and some did not.

However, since I began my treatment with Suboxone several years ago, my symptoms have been more significantly reduced than they ever were on any other medication. Suboxone makes me feel the way I think I am supposed to feel. It makes me feel normal, in a good way. I feel able to control myself and accomplish the things I desire to achieve. I feel motivated and confident. My moods seem within a more normal range. I can be sad or happy, frustrated or anxious without losing control of my behavior. In short, I feel that I can manage and enjoy my life, achieve independence, and build trusting, healthy relationships.

Since I have been on Suboxone treatment, my progress has been significant. I have renewed interest in hobbies, work, and family life. Additionally, I have achieved complete independence and self-sufficiency for the first time in my life. Furthermore, I not only support myself but also provide for my girlfriend and her young son! Research is underway for the use of Suboxone for depression and other psychiatric disorders.

Medication-assisted treatment, a term used to describe

addiction treatment that includes the use of medications like Suboxone or Methadone, is a strategy used to reduce the negative impacts of drug use on addicts, families, and societies. Harm reduction is an approach to drug use and management that tries to maintain realistic expectations and perspectives about drug use and its effects on the individual and society. The movement recognizes that people will use drugs no matter how strict laws or consequences are. Harm reduction considers drug prohibition to be a losing battle that results in more harm than good. Prohibition takes control out of the hands of doctors and other educated professionals with mostly good intentions. It puts all the control in the hands of criminals.

In my opinion, drug laws are harmful because they spend enormous amounts of money to incarcerate and punish people who would commit no other crime besides consuming drugs. This produces more crime because, after serving time, these individuals come out into society with a criminal record and habits of survival not conducive to mainstream life. Harm reduction primarily seeks to reduce and minimize harm caused by, and associated with, drug use through various strategies, including medication-assisted treatment or maintenance therapy. This strategy replaces harmful, dangerous, unstable street drugs with less harmful alternatives. Harm reduction strategies scaffold the addict's efforts toward progress and stability. It is important to remain open-minded and conversational about the potential of harm reduction efforts in our society. Some countries have even legalized heroin as a treatment option for people who are not successful with use of Suboxone or methadone.

Maintenance therapy drugs give people who are going to use opioids a safer, legal, affordable alternative, which allows opioid users to carry on relatively normal lives. Instead of using heroin supplied by a drug dealer that could be cut with dangerous substances, opioid users receive a controlled and safely measured dosage of a prescribed alternative, like methadone, in a controlled environment.

Suboxone is another drug used in maintenance therapy. It is a take-home medication given in one-month-supply increments. Because of its relative safety compared to methadone, patients are empowered to manage their own treatment, daily, with less direct supervision. Patients who participate in medication-assisted treatment therapy do not have to worry about the risks associated with obtaining illegal drugs on the street. This alleviates stress and establishes a foundation for progress. Patients can stop worrying about repercussions (like arrest and incarceration) and shift their energy and focus toward matters of family, work, and the demands of a more conventional lifestyle.

Another benefit of medication-assisted treatment is the affordability when compared to illegal drug use. When opioid users obtain heroin on the streets, they pay a premium because of the risks involved for dealers, and based on supply and demand —which can be unpredictable and inconsistent. This leads people who are dependent on opioids to commit crimes in order to fund their habit. As the addiction progresses, users deplete their personal resources and turn to crime, increasing their risk of death, incarceration, and alienation by family members. Stress and shame spiral. The cycle becomes a freighted tumble into a destination of destruction.

Patients who participate in medication-assisted treatment with Suboxone are monitored by health care professionals and spend time in substance treatment classes instead of spending outrageous amounts of time in the culture of drug dealers, untreated addicts, and criminal activity. Not having to worry about where their next fix will come from alleviates an overwhelming burden for a dependent drug user, facilitating the recovery process and positively reinforcing the decision to continue participating fully and consistently in treatment and recovery.

On the other hand, heroin obtained on the street comes in unpredictable strengths, depending on the source and how it was made. With no regulation to ensure consistency of strength, illegally obtaining heroin from drug dealers and using it becomes a game of Russian roulette. Street drugs are not controlled. Therefore, they are made in a variety of ways and mixed with a variety of other substances. This dilution of pure heroin and other street drugs is called cutting. It is one of the main reasons so many people die of overdoses.

One extremely dangerous drug that is used to cut heroin is fentanyl. Fentanyl is a synthetic opioid that is fifty to one hundred times more potent than morphine. It is also significantly more potent than heroin. Currently, there are several fentanyl analogs. These substances act in similar ways to fentanyl, but currently, they are not detectable on common drug tests. When addicts look for opioids, they don't exactly get to choose or even know exactly what they're getting. With these drugs being so powerful in very small amounts, risk of overdose is high. Additionally, some of these analogs are even more highly addictive than fentanyl, which is already much more addictive than heroin. One fentanyl analog, carfentanyl, is estimated to be ten thousand times more potent than morphine (O'Donnell et al., 2018).

Because these synthetic analog opioids vary widely in strength and purity, it is critical that addicts know about safer choices through medication-assisted treatment. If you or someone you know abuses opioids, there is hope for recovery. Suboxone has improved my life and helped me to be more of the person I want to be. Let's join together and spread the word about medication-assisted treatment. It saves lives!

FINANCIAL ASSISTANCE TO ADDICTS

When this topic came up in a conversation with a friend, I was surprised that I had not thought more about it or addressed it directly in some other part of this book. Financial issues are significant in the lives of addicts, whether they are actively abusing drugs or stable in recovery. Illegal drugs and prescribed medications both require monetary resources. The expenses related to drug use and recovery programs can both weigh heavy on an addict who tries to accomplish independence.

When family members watch this struggle and see a recovering addict making progress, they may be tempted to offer money to help the addict reach certain goals. Most people can follow the logic not to give money to a person actively abusing drugs. But the difficulty comes in the other realm, when the addict is in recovery and struggling to make ends meet because of the heavy financial burden of medication-assisted treatment.

So, I will tell you what I have concluded from my experience. Giving money to an addict to help them get ahead can trigger irresistible temptation—even to an addict who is doing well in their recovery. One of the motivators for remaining in recovery is financial stability. But if an addict has funds above what they need for immediate expenses, their risk of relapsing increases because of the overwhelming temptation to experience the intense high their addiction craves.

An alternative is to cover specific expenses, like new tires or dental care, by paying the bill directly. Helping an addict *save for the future* by giving them money is a risky venture that could lead to relapse and loss of hard-earned money. You may think, as I did, that giving them a nest egg will alleviate stress related to living from paycheck to paycheck. But everything must be reconsidered in light of the addiction. If you want an addict to have funds for emergencies, save the money for them instead of giving it to them. Otherwise, your generosity and good intentions might enable the addict to resume or continue abusing drugs.

LETTER TO THE READER
BY SIMMS

Dear Reader,

Thank you for reading our story! The revision process took longer than we imagined, but I hope you found it worth the wait. Some of you might be wondering what I have been up to lately —besides helping my mom revise this book.

I was released from prison on August 7, 2020. Then, I completed parole in May 2021. Since my release, I have been working with the North Carolina Harm Reduction Coalition to help people suffering from addiction all across North Carolina. I do peer outreach for them, helping connect people in active addiction with medical and psychiatric services to help them survive, work through, and overcome their addictions so they can move on and create the life they want to live.

I was invited to participate in a medical-psychiatric addiction study conducted by Duke University to create new programs that connect addicts with relevant medical services they need by consolidating various treatment initiatives to make them available through medication-assisted treatment programs (such as methadone and Suboxone clinics). I am passionate and outspoken in my advocacy of drug law reform, addiction reform, addiction treatment, and harm reduction. And I continue to speak publicly and write about the issues surrounding these subjects, hoping to further these causes.

I also research and study new drugs and addiction trends in pursuit of my goal to publish some of my work in reputable academic journals. Presently, I am preparing to move into a new place with my girlfriend as we prepare to celebrate our one-year anniversary.

Finally, I am proud to say I have personally saved over one hundred people from opioid overdose by administering the antidote naloxone and providing rescue breaths to the victims until their condition stabilized. I am thankful for the opportunity to speak out about my challenges related to addiction and support other addicts as they navigate the rocky road of recovery.

Warmest regards,

Simms

~

We hope your reading of this book has been a positive experience. Please consider reviewing *Letters Behind Bars: A Mother-Son Memoir* to help others find our story. We appreciate your feedback and support!

Visit www.CinnaminHerring.com and check out my blog where you can read more of my writing and find other surprises. Enter your email at the bottom of my website home page to receive occasional notifications about new content. Thank you!

MAJOR EVENTS TIMELINE

January 2015

- Simms was arrested and incarcerated in New Hanover County Jail on numerous drug-related charges, including drug trafficking.

April 2015

- Simms's father, Ben, passed away from sudden cardiac arrest.

September 2015

- Simms's bond was reduced from $125,000 to $5,000.
- Cinnamin bailed him out of jail to await trial.

October 2016

- The courts convicted Simms of drug-related felonies and sentenced him to probation with suspended-sentence contingencies.

December 2017

- Simms was charged with possession with intent to sell Schedule VI substances.

January 2018

- Simms was charged with possession of a Schedule II substance.

May 2018

- Simms was charged with possession with intent to sell a Schedule III substance.
- Simms was arrested and incarcerated without bond in New Hanover County Jail.

November 2018

- Simms's case was settled with consolidation of crimes.
- The court ordered him to serve a suspended sentence for his 2016 conviction.
- Simms was transferred from New Hanover County Jail to Polk Correctional Institution for processing into the North Carolina Prison System.

January 2019

- Simms was transferred to Alexander Correctional Institution (a close-custody maximum security facility) after a brief stay at Central Prison, where he underwent a medical procedure related to injuries from a fight at Polk.

August 2019

- Simms was relocated to Mountain View Correctional Institution based on his change from close custody to medium custody.

September 2019

- Simms was transferred to Pender Correctional Institution to participate in a drug education program.

December 2019

- Simms was transferred back to Mountain View Correctional Center following his completion of the drug education program at Pender Correctional Institution.

August 7, 2020

- Simms was released from prison on parole.

May 2021

- Simms successfully completed parole.

REFERENCES

Huhn AS, Hobelmann JG, Oyler GA, Strain EC. Protracted Renal Clearance of Fentanyl in Persons with Opioid Use Disorder. *Drug Alcohol Depend.* September 2020. 214:108147.

NIDA. 2021, June 1. Fentanyl DrugFacts. Retrieved from https://www.drugabuse.gov/publications/drugfacts/fentanyl on September 6, 2021

NIDA. 2021, June 1. Naloxone DrugFacts. Retrieved from https://www.drugabuse.gov/publications/drugfacts/naloxone on September 3, 2021

O'Donnell J, Gladden RM, Mattson CL, Kariisa M. Notes from the Field: Overdose Deaths with Carfentanil and Other Fentanyl Analogs Detected–10 States, July 2016–June 2017. *MMWR Morb Mortal Wkly Rep.* July 2018. 67(27): 767–768.

Velander JR. Suboxone: Rationale, Science, Misconceptions. *Ochsner J.* Spring 2018. 18(1): 23–29.